"Dr. Tom Barnette ... selor, and humble servant at Believers Baptist Church in Pattison, Texas. Tom has been faithful to skill himself in order to better meet the needs of those within the church and in the community at large."
*Dr. Darrell Horn, Executive Director of the San Felipe Baptist Association in Rosenberg, Texas*

"Dr. Barnette's book is a thoughtful and down-to-earth exploration of the Harvest Principle as it is found throughout Scripture. In the midst of a culture dedicated to immediacy and impulse, Dr. Tom explains a different path: a path where seeds are sown, watered, and watched patiently, with hope, until they finally bloom into life-giving fruit. He points out that many of us know our problems as well as our solutions, but we seem to consistently fail in embracing and acting out the solutions. He proposes that what we are missing is discipline and consistency, and his Biblical application is *The Rule of 52*: breaking a solution into small steps that we can accomplish on a weekly basis. Dr. Tom shows us our inner conflicts using simple language and effective stories from his own life as a counselor, and he never comes across as prideful or arrogant. Instead he allows us to laugh at ourselves while pointing out common traps we all fall into. He ultimately offers us hope in the form of a workable plan that is accessible to anyone.

I found myself challenged to be faithful in the small things as I read through the book. As a young man it is easy for me to be drawn into the false thinking that everything has to be large and immediate. But Dr. Tom's book has encouraged me to instead be faithful; to have the right trajectory and heart; to desire to change in ways that allow me to love God and others more; and to be patient while God works those changes. I enjoyed the many practical applications he gives, and I am currently trying to enact them in my own life. His thoughts on affirming those who God has placed in our lives were especially convicting, and I have taken it to heart to try to spend quality time and continually speak affirmation to the people I love."
*Travis Gaspar*

# The Rule of 52

*Dr Tom Barrett*

*God Bless you*
*to Know you*

*EpH 2:8*

*The Rule of 52*

Published by Lucid Books in Brenham, TX.
www.LucidBooks.net

First Printing 2010

ISBN-13: 978-0-9789265-4-0
ISBN-10: 0-9789265-4-4

Special Sales: Most Lucid Books titles are available in special quantity discounts. Custom imprinting or excerpting can also be done to fit special needs. Contact Lucid Books at info@lucidbooks.net.

# The Rule of 52

Tom Barnette

LUCIDBOOKS

*To My Family,*
*Belinda my Wife*
*My Children*
*Tommie Alice, Jonathan Clayton, LeeAnn Marie,*
*And*
*My Beloved Church family.*

# Contents

# Foreword

The *Rule of 52* is an innovative advancement to applying power, knowledge, and success to our lives today. The book is contemporary and thought provoking. The guidelines teach individuals and families how to be successful in spite of the 21st century's complexities and problems. All people everywhere would like to be mentally, spiritually, and physically successful. The 21st century family's success is in rapid decline and under constant bombardment from the world. *Rule of 52* is a new insightful and fresh system of success in a world filled with failure.

Dr. Tom Barnette's book teaches you to see the world differently through new realistic and permanent success. *Rule of 52* is a literal Christian, eye-opening experience. The illustrations are wonderful and heart felt, a real down-to-earth reading experience. The book is refreshingly clear, yet exceptionally thought provoking.

*Rule of 52* is a simplistic approach to a total life and family success. The book will help direct and teach you how to stay permanently successful. Lasting permanent success should be the experience of each and every Christian. The book is straightforward and user friendly for everyday life. Dr. Tom's book is a vital guideline to families and individuals in search of dynamic new solutions to the same old life problems. God created you to be successful in marriage, parenting, business, and individual life.

*Dr. John Bisagno*

Dr. John Bisagno is Pastor Emeritus of the 22,000-member Houston's First Baptist Church. His remarkable 30 years of ministry at Houston's First Baptist is summed up in Rick Warren's words: "There are some great pastors that excel in one particular area. But John has excelled at it all." It is precisely this multi-gifted aspect that propelled Dr. John to be a dynamic evangelist, compassionate shepherd, and strong leader. Dr. John Bisagno is the author of 30 books including *Love Is Something You Do.*

# Preface

The Rule of 52 does not help you help yourself; it directs, tutors, and guides you to the Will of God for your Family Life Success.

## Combination to Unlock Lasting Success

*The Big Question to ask yourself is do you want to be successful? Do you want to be successful at just a few things? If you want to be successful at all things, is this a realistic idea? Do you think it is God's will for Christians to be really successful?*

*The Rule of 52* is the key to unlocking your permanent and lasting life success.

The reality is that each and every time you go to open a combination lock you have to work the same combination to get the lock open. *The Rule of 52* works the same way to achieve the desired results (success) to open the lock (problem).

The solution does not change. Successful sowing and reaping are the repetitive combination of life. You and I will change, but the problem has to be worked each and every time in exactly the same way. Self help is out and God's will is in because it works. Knowing God's will and applying God's will are two different things. *The Rule of 52* does not help you help yourself; it directs you to the Will of God for your life.

God's law of sowing and reaping does not change. You change! The success process does not. Harvest Rule one states, "You reap what you sow." Have you ever asked the question what is the will of God for my life? Do you ever plan to be out of God's will?

Do you accidentally slip out of God's will? No matter how far or how fast you travel in the wrong direction, you will never reach the right location. You cannot travel in the wrong direction and get to the right place. Let's apply wrong directions to the other parts of life. You cannot spend your way out of debt. You cannot borrow your way out of debt. The only way to get out of debt is to earn your way out of debt. You can't yell at your children enough to make them behave. You cannot argue with your spouse and fix your marriage. So, why do you keep doing the same failed thing over and over again?

At the end of the right direction, blessings are waiting. The only way to be successful is to go in the right direction in each and every area of your life.

By learning the guidelines and principles in *The Rule of 52* you can become successful in life, family, and business. The question is if this process is so darn simple, then why can't I make the course corrections to be successful? Knowing the right direction and crossing the ocean without a compass to guide you is almost impossible. *The Rule of 52* is the help you need to apply a successful directional change today! It's your journey to success. Why not start today?

# Introduction

When applying The Rule of 52 to your individual life, it always begins with a question. Could you lose one pound per month? Most people who are overweight are more than aware they are overweight! The person knows the problem! The person knows that with diet and exercise he can lose weight; so he knows the answer. If the answer is so simple, why not just lose the weight? That is the 10% of the answer that escapes us.

Let's ask *The Rule of 52* questions. Could a person lose 1 pound per month? This is a very reasonable goal for most people. The answer is yes! A person can lose 1 pound per month! That would be approximately 1 pound per month or 12 pounds per year or 24 pounds in two years. What would you physically look like in two years if you lost 24 pounds?

I tell all students of all ages going to college to take a copy of their birth certificate with them and tape it to their bathroom mirror and look at it each morning. Then make the following statement: "I can get older with an education or I can get older without an education; but either way, I am going to get older." The problem with most solutions is that we are unrealistic with our expectations. Reality has to play a large role in success.

Could you save $5 dollars per week for 52 weeks? That would equal $260 dollars at the end of one year. At the end of 20 years, you would have $5,200 dollars. Would that amount of cash make a difference in your life right now? Would you ever really miss the $5 dollars each week? What if you could save $100 dollars per week? At the end the year, you would have $5,200 dollars; and at the end of

20 years, the total would be $ 104,000 dollars. If you had that much cash in the bank right now, would it make a difference in your life? The fact is that you can get older without savings or you can get older with savings in the bank; but the fact is, you will get older!

| | |
|---|---|
| The Rule of 1: | Something you do once a year |
| The Rule of 12: | Something you do once a month |
| The Rule of 52: | Something you do once a week |
| The Rule of 104: | Something you do only on weekends |
| The Rule of 261: | Something you do only on weekdays |
| The Rule of 365: | Something you do once a day |

*The Rule of 52* can be applied to many things in our lives. *The Rule of 52* is about life's successes and sowing the seeds of success in others. *The Rule of 52* is not a course in time management; it is about successful life relationships. General George S. Patton said, *"Never tell people how to do things. Tell them what to do and they will surprise you with their ingenuity."*

# Chapter 1

## Each Breath You Take Is of Equal Importance

*From your first breath to the very last exhale, each one is equally as important to you as the last.*

The big questions to ask yourself are do you want to be successful? Do you want to be successful at just a few things? If you want to be successful at all things, is this a realistic idea? Everything you have ever been successful at had a starting point and started with a plan. There is a picket fence on top of a hill. The fence is weathered and it has broken boards. The fence has no beginning and no end; it is just stuck on top of the hill. You have been assigned the task of repairing the fence, and you have all the necessary tools. You have the planks, the nails, the paint, and a limitless amount of time to fix the fence. The question is, "Where do you start?" The answer is, "What does it matter?!" Due to the fact that the entire fence is in need of repair, you simply must pick a place and start. Whatever you do to repair the fence that day creates a 100% improvement. Likewise, whatever you do the next day will create another 100% improvement. Ultimately, it is your choice of how hard you want to work and how far you wish to take the fence repair. It is up to you! The amount of time, energy, and effort will be directly proportional to the outcome. So, what one thing can you do today to start fixing your broken fences?

If you drive a car, you should have a spare tire. Why do you carry a spare tire? The logical answer is in case you have a flat. Many people today do not know how to change a flat tire; much less have the desire to. In Houston, Texas, there are a vast number of tire stores for a very specific reason. That reason is the construction industry combined with a great deal of rain and mud. Construction trucks roll onto the construction site where mud, nails and debris stick to the tires. Then the big wheeled trucks roll down the road and deposit the mud, nails, and debris all over the highways and byways; thus creating flat tires. A whole commercial industry has been developed around the idea of tire replacement. There are specialists who solely handle tire repair and replacement. Enough rambling about tires, but it is essential that you understand the reality.

If you drive a car, at some point in time you will have a flat tire. The first fact: flat tires are always inconvenient. The second fact: you are never happy about having a flat tire. The third fact: there is some feeling of relief and satisfaction when you open the trunk and the spare tire is really there and not flat. Finally, after changing the flat tire with the temporary fix, you have a sense of fulfillment that comes with accomplishing a problem-solving task and driving safely on your way. The majority of people can handle one flat tire problem at a time. Panic occurs when your car has four flat tires and the spare tire is flat. Now the situation seems hopeless and you are in desperate need of assistance. The problem of four flat tires represents a reality that you cannot fix for yourself. You require help just to get the car to the tire hospital. In a similar way, most people know 90% of their problems and 90% of their solutions. What escapes them is the 10%, and that is what is called *The Rule of 52* **which provides the steps to success. It is no secret.** *The Rule of 52* deals with that which people are not willing, ready, or able to deal with in their life **events.** If you seem to fail over and over again, even when you know what you want and how to win; if all your attempts come up short, then *The Rule of 52* is for you!

*Sometimes when you plan to buy a loaf of bread, you find the most delightful package of cinnamon rolls out of place. You should buy them at all cost. They were just waiting for you! We know many of our problems and we know many of the answers to our problems. But knowing how to make the solutions become part of reality escapes each of us.* Being the solution to the problem is the success of *The Rule of 52.*

## The Man and His Coffee

Have you ever made a cup of coffee? If yes, then you are familiar with the rules of coffee making. It's true, even making a cup of coffee has a set of rules. Each day a man got up and poured himself a cup of coffee. Next, he added a little cream and sugar, then a little more cream and sugar, and a little more cream and sugar. Soon the coffee was too sweet and too creamy to drink, so he just poured it down the drain. The man did this each and every morning. Likewise, the man had a neighbor who would wake up and also pour himself a cup of coffee. Into the cup of coffee he would add a little cream and a little sugar. Then he would take a spoon and stir it up. Paul writes to a young Timothy in II Timothy 1:6a, *"remember that you should stir up the gift of God, which is in you."* From the very moment of your conception, you are created with everything you will ever be. You are born complete with eye color, hair color, skin tone, and everything you will ever need to be completed. All you have to do is grow and develop. Jesus said, "I will make the hay, you just show up to the harvest." God already put everything in you that you will ever need. Simply stir up that which is within you!

# Chapter 2

## Harvest Rule One:
## You Reap What You Sow

*The only two things worth standing in line for are graduation and ice cream.*

Winning is not a sometime thing; it's an all the time thing. One of the most inspirational moments in football history was in a 1970 speech by Vince Lombardi, Coach of the Green Bay Packers from 1959 to 1967. Coach Lombardi turned a persistent losing team into a juggernaut, winning NFL titles in 1961, 1962, and 1965 in addition to Super Bowls I and II in 1966 and 1967. Today Coach Lombardi is the standard against which all coaches are measured. What is your life measured by?

Vince Lombardi said, "Winning is not a sometime thing; it's an all the time thing. You don't win once in a while; you don't do things right once in a while; you do them right all the time. Winning is a habit. Unfortunately, so is losing." Winning is a habit, so is losing. On average it takes about 7 days to memorize something and 30 days to develop a habit. All habits require work. We spend time and money developing habits. Habits require commitment and concentration, and no habit is developed by accident. No one accidentally learns to smoke or drink. No one accidentally learns a new phone number or how to drive. The bottom line is that people develop habits because they want to!

Vince Lombardi also said, "There is no room for second place. There is only one place in my game, and that's first place. It is and always has been an American zeal to be first in anything we do, and to win, and to win, and to win." Who came in second place three Super Bowls ago? The answer is, "Who cares?"

In Ecclesiastes 9:10, wise old Solomon wrote, *"Whatever your hand finds to do, do it with all your might; for there is no activity or planning or knowledge or wisdom in Sheol where you are going. 11 I again saw under the sun that the race is not to the swift and the battle is not to the warriors, and neither is bread to the wise nor wealth to the discerning nor favor to men of ability; for time and chance overtake them all."*

This scripture lines up with another Lombardi teaching: "Every time a football player goes to apply his trade, he's got to play from the ground up-from the soles of his feet right up to his head. Every inch of him has to play. Some guys play with their heads. That's O.K. You've got to be smart to be number one in any business. But more importantly, you've got to play with your heart, with every fiber of your body. If you're lucky enough to find a guy with a lot of head and a lot of heart, he's never going to come off the field second."

Winners always want the ball and want the game to keep going. The thing about football is that each and every player on the field knows how to throw, catch, tackle, block, hit, take a hit, and run, so all knowledge is equal. Not all work ethic or desire is equal. It is a reality of life that men are competitive, and the most competitive games draw the most competitive men. They are there to compete. Every player needs to know the rules and objectives when they play the game. The object is to play fairly, squarely, by the rules, and still win. And in truth, I've never known a man worth his salt who, in the long run, deep down in his heart, didn't appreciate the grind and the discipline. There is something in good men that really yearns for discipline and the harsh reality of head to head combat.

My high school coach would say, "I'll tell you when you're running too fast, hitting too hard, and winning by too many points. Until then, keep doing everything with all your might. I don't want to hear, 'I'm trying, Coach.' That kind of talk is for losers. You're doing it or you're not doing it. So figure out what you're doing wrong and fix it!"

Lombardi said, "I don't say these things because I believe in the 'brute' nature of man or that man must be brutalized to be combative. I believe in God, and I believe in human decency. But I firmly believe that any man's finest hour, the greatest fulfillment of all that he holds dear, is that moment when he has worked his heart out in a good cause and lies exhausted on the field of battle."

Vince Lombardi summed up *The Rule of 52*, which is, "to know the rules and objectives when they get in the game. The object is to win fairly, squarely, by the rules, but win." I must confess, as a high school football player our coach had this Lombardi speech on an old 45 LP, and he played it over and over again in the locker room before games. I thought a lot about the statement, and I noted to myself that not everybody played by the rules. It was very apparent that not everyone had the same objectives. They were also trying to win, but they could with or without the rules. Thus began the birth of the inspiration of *The Rule of 52*.

# Crack Addict

*The only direction worth traveling is the one that will take you somewhere better than where you are in the present! Sometimes, as Robert Frost said, this is "the road less traveled and that made all the difference."*

Many years ago, I was a volunteer counselor with a local shelter. My job was simply to observe and assist the counselors in training so they could all become mature counselors. It was a men's shelter which specialized in alcohol and drug treatment. The first step for all new clients was the intake room. It was a simple room with one glass door, two folding tables, chairs, and two seated counselors ready to receive new clients. I was standing in the back of the room behind the two counselors, watching and listening.

A tall, thin man hesitantly walked through the glass door. He wore a London Fog style trench coat that was once costly, but was now threadbare and grimy with wear. He had a salt and pepper stubbly beard and matted hair under his baseball cap. His face and hands were dark from baking in the sun, but his sockless ankles were white as a ghost. His face had the hollow look of hunger and hopelessness. He walked up to the inexperienced counselor and said his name was Ben. Ben decided to give the place a chance if the counselor thought it would help! The counselor assured him that it would make all the difference, but first he would need some basic information. Ben agreed and began to tell his story. Everyone always has a story and Ben's story was all too familiar.

Hopelessness dribbled out of his mouth as Ben shared his life. He once had a wife and two little girls, but he had long since stopped crying over his loss. He just lived in the vacuum of loss called his life. All of Ben's cares were lost with each hit of crack. Ben shared that he once had a career in the local TV media world, but he had attended one too many parties. The party scene of the Hollywood society seduced him, and he started using crack cocaine. Ben lost himself in that underworld. The young counselor assured Ben that the shelter could help.

Ben stated that he had a crack pipe in his pocket and had planned to simply go out and try to smoke himself to death. He had decided he would give the shelter a try first. He had no hope in his statement. Ben held firmly to the belief in his personal friend known as failure. He took the pipe out of his pocket and showed it to the young counselor. The counselor looked at the pipe and said, "You will have to give the drugs to me right now before I admit you to the shelter." Ben looked at the pipe, then at the young counselor, then back at the pipe before starting for the glass door. I dashed to the table, wanting to pop the counseling youngster in the back of head, but I refrained. I slid right over the top of the table and positioned myself between Ben and the glass door. I said, "Hi Ben, I'm Tom. Please give me just one moment of your time and then you can go."

Ben thought about it for a second and shrugged his shoulders. He did not have anything else to do except smoke himself to death. I held out my hand, making a fist, and said, "Ben, in this hand I have your wife, your two little girls, your job, and your life. If you will let me, I would like to give them back to you. I would like to put them into your hand right now." His eyes opened with hope and a toothless smile emerged. I then said, "But you will have to trade me. You put that crack pipe in my hand and I will put your little girls back in your hand." Ben took out the crack cocaine and the pipe to place them in my hands. Then I took his hand and led him back to the treatment center.

Today, Ben is clean and sober. He re-established a relationship with his little girls and has worked many years as a volunteer at the shelter. Ben has put his hand out many times to the broken hearted and addicted; trading a handful of hope for their broken lives and hopeless dreams.

God has given man eternal, absolute rules of the harvest, as well as rules of sowing and reaping before harvest time. These rules are like the physical laws of gravity. Gravity is eternal from the creation of God. The same formula for gravity can be used to calculate your weight on Mars as on Earth. Gravity is universal; it can't be repealed by man. Gravity can be calculated, observed, tested, and experienced, but it cannot be explained. Gravity affects all ages from the dawn of time to now. Gravity is not prejudiced. It has no bias, and it is used by both good and evil. Its effects are always felt but never noticed; unless you are skydiving or bungee jumping. Then gravity plays a big part of reality.

Sir Isaac Newton wrote, "But though the system of revealed truth which [the Bible] contains is, like that of the universe, concealed from common observation, yet the labors of the centuries have established its Divine origin, and developed in all its order and beauty the great plan of human restoration." Newton, the Christian, knew that God reveals Himself through scientific, physical, universal absolutes and truths.

## God's Truth Starts with the Planting of a Seed! This Is Scientific Truth

Paul writes to the Galatians in Galatians 6:6-8: *"But let him that is taught in the word communicate unto him that teaches in all good things. Be not deceived; God is not mocked: for what ever man sows that shall he also reap. For he that Sows unto his own flesh shall of the flesh reap corruption; but he that Sows unto the Spirit shall of the Spirit reap eternal life."*

This is a simple truth that you have heard from every grandparent to Poor Richard's Almanac. "You reap what you sow." This quote from the Bible has been taught as a behavioral word of warning to children. The lesson has been presented like the boogie man to people of all ages in hope of a behavioral foreshadowing. The reaping and sowing lesson that is handed down has been relegated to a homespun piece of philosophy quoted by Grandpa to the wayward child.

Reaping and sowing are the cornerstone principles of *The Rule of 52*. The harvest laws are God's formula for success. God the Father is the author and finisher of success. It is essential to understand the formula of the harvest laws to be able to apply the success principles of *The Rule of 52*.

The dictionary's definition of sow is to place (seeds) in or on the ground for future growth.

Sowing is an old English term from the 1300's that means to plant a seed, yet it encompasses so much more. For thousands of years, seeds have been exceedingly valuable. Each seed could mean the difference between starving and survival, especially in the ancient world. Sowing was not just planting; it dealt with preserving the seed until the season was right to plant. There were people called sowers who were specialists in planting. They prepared the field and understood how to plant with success. They would stand watch over the crop by day and by night, keeping the birds from eating all the seeds and the livestock from grazing on the tender buds. The idea of sowing is simple. It means to physically plant a seed. Have you ever known someone with a green thumb? My grandmother could plant a dead stick in the ground and grow a tree. She was a sower of all things beautiful and good that came from the earth.

The dictionary's definition of reap is to gather; to obtain; to receive as a reward or harvest, or as the fruit of labor or of works. Reaping was a separate trade, and a specialized activity in the harvest. Reaping is simply understood as the act of picking or gathering a crop. The term reaper or harvester is used universally in the Bible for all forms of picking crops. The word reaping may equally refer to a large harvest or picking one single apple from a tree. The term reaper also refers to the person who picked the crops. Using the term harvester or reaper is like saying attorney or lawyer; same person different term. The term reaper originated from the hand tool called a sickle or a reaper.

The absolute truth about sowing and reaping is that the activity of planting occurs at the beginning of the season, and the harvesting always happens at the end of the season. God had a two part economic system from the very dawn of creation. The rules of the harvest occur all over the earth in both man and nature.

## Combination Lock

You are given a combination lock with 50 numbers. You are asked to simply unlock it by guessing the combination of 6 different numbers. If you worked the problem 24 hours a day, 7 days per week, and if the very last combination you guessed was the right one, it would take you many hours since there are thousands of different possible combinations in the series.

Instead, you are given the series of the 6 different numbers needed to unlock the combination. You can now open the lock in just a few moments. You now have the key to work the problem. The new knowledge you possess allows you to successfully unlock the problem. The reality is that each and every time you go to open the combination lock, you have to work the same problem with the same series of numbers to get the lock open. *The Rule of 52* works the same way to achieve the desired results (success) to open the lock (problem). The solution does not change.

Successful sowing and reaping are the repetitive combination of life. You and I will change, but the problem has to be worked each and every time in exactly the same way. God's laws of sowing and reaping are absolute. You change, the process does not!

Hebrews 13:8 states, *"Jesus Christ is the same yesterday, today, and forever."* This is Harvest Rule One: "You reap what you sow."

# Chapter 3

## Harvest Rule Two:
## You Reap Exactly What You Sow

> *If I gave you a glass of water to drink, but first I spit into the glass, what part of the water is not corrupted or separate from the spit? Which part would you drink?*

J esus said in Matthew 7:16
*"You shall know them by their fruits. Do men gather grapes of thorns, or figs of thistles? Even so every good tree brings forth good fruit; but a corrupt tree brings forth evil fruit. A good tree cannot bring forth evil fruit; neither can a corrupt tree bring forth good fruit. Every tree that brings not forth good fruit is cut down, and cast into the fire. Wherefore by their fruits ye shall know them."*

If you plant an apple tree, you get apples. If you plant a rose bush, you get roses. If you plant problems, you will grow problems, and so on and so on. What you plant is what you will grow. If you plant good things, then in time you will receive the blessing of good things. If you plant bad things, then you will grow bad things. If you keep planting the same stuff, you will just get more of the same stuff.

I consider it a bit disturbing that 80% of all cancer patients who smoked prior to cancer once they are in remission from cancer keep right on smoking. Many people plant evil in their lives and relationships expecting good to grow. A quote attributed to Ben Franklin states, "I respectfully suggest that the definition of insanity is doing the same thing over and over and expecting it to come out differently." Yet we still spend all of our money and expect to save. We run up credit card charges, pay high interest for our toys, and expect no debt. Individuals distrust, yet expect trust in return. People are sarcastic and still expect a kind word from others. Men throughout the world sow evil discourse and expect peace. The only real expectation should be that we will reap exactly what we sow. Why should you lose weight if your diet consists of donuts, soft drinks, and fast food with no exercise?

## Harvest Rules One and Two: You Reap What You Sow and You Reap Exactly What You Sow

I was 18 and had recently graduated from high school. I was one of 23,000 members of First Baptist Church of Houston, and my pastor was Dr. John Bisagno. Dr. Bisagno is one of the true visionaries of the 20th and 21st centuries, and he was preaching and teaching through the book of Revelation. I was privileged to soak up the knowledge of my great pastor and friend. I was newly licensed to the ministry in the summer of 1980. I decided to earnestly start a Bible study in my home on Tuesday nights and invite all my heathen friends from high school. The curriculum was easy. Whatever Dr. John preached on Sunday, I taught on Tuesday, and boy did I sound smart! At least as long as the young people attending did not ask too many questions.

Each week my audience included Spring Branch High School football players (Once a Bear always a Bear), their girlfriends, as well as cowboys and all their host of different girlfriends. I hosted the Bible study in the living room of my home. Over the summer, the crowd grew to more than 30 people, mostly graduated seniors. Most, if not all of my friends had never attended church except on traditional holidays and weddings. Studying the Book of Revelation was fascinating and challenging. The Bible study would culminate with everybody going to the local Billy Bob's Dance Hall, Beer Emporium, and Drunken Fest. This was always a very Spiritual way to top off the Bible study. The group's motto should have been, "A beer in one hand and a Bible in the back seat of the truck."

At that time, First Baptist of Houston held an old-fashioned, Holy Spirit-filled, and powerful week long crusade in a football stadium. Dr. John was preaching the crusade in 1980. The next Tuesday night of the Bible study, after everyone had arrived and the beer was iced down in the back of the trucks, I announced that we were all going to the crusade. The only question the group asked was, "What's a crusade?" My explanation was, "It's a big Bible study with music!" With that explanation, 32 teenagers piled into their trucks and drove to the stadium, just like they were going to a football game followed by a trip to the dance hall. It was in that stadium that 30 teens ran face first into the reality of the Cross of Jesus Christ. For the first time they heard the life saving message of the truth.

Dr. John preached an excellent but elegantly simple message. He then asked if anyone would come to know new life through Jesus Christ. With the first call to come forward and accept Jesus, I had the most Spiritually wonderful, jaw-dropping experience of my life. Thirty-one unchurched, unrepentant, unsaved teenagers stood up and walked right down to the front of the stage and accepted Jesus Christ as their personal Lord and Savior.

The following Sunday, 26 of my friends were baptized. The summer came to a quick end as all summers do, and our group moved on to our respective future lives and colleges. I have not seen most of those friends since that time. One of those friends has already gone to be with the Lord. As I write this book, exactly 30 years have passed with the reassuring knowledge that my dear friends who shaped my life will live again with my King.

Flash forward in time from 1980 to 2001. Dr. John Bisagno, now retired from First Baptist Church of Houston, was serving as the interim pastor position for a church in the town in which I resided. This provided a wonderful opportunity for my family to experience my great pastor and dear friend.

On our first visit to the church, my youngest daughter, LeeAnn, was 9 years old. The first time she heard Dr. John preach she said, "Daddy, that man preaches just like you." She did not know it at the time, but she paid me one of the best compliments of my life. I tried to explain to her that it was the other way around. LeeAnn and I had been discussing salvation, sin, and baptism for the past three years. Even at her young age, she had an amazing grasp of the real meaning of Jesus Christ. However, she was hesitant to walk to the front of the church and formally profess Jesus Christ as her Savior. She understood that before she could be baptized she had to make her public profession of faith.

Over the next several weeks, I had the privilege of becoming re-acquainted with my pastor and friend while my family attended the worship services. At one service, Dr. John began to preach, and it was the exact same message from the crusade 30 years ago. All the power of the Holy Spirit filled my heart, and I thought of all my friends from long ago who had accepted Jesus before men. I knew that for some of them, it might have been their one and only chance to become a Christian.

At the close of the service, Dr. John gave an invitation for the lost to receive Christ. At that moment a little hand slipped into my hand, and LeeAnn asked me to go forward with her so that she could receive Jesus Christ as her Lord and Savior. In that moment, the reality of God's promise came to life for me, and I understood the clear and present message of God the Father. I really had reaped what I sowed all those years ago. Blessed be His name!

The apostle Paul sums it up best in Galatians 6:7. *"Do not be deceived, God is not mocked; for whatever a man sows this he will also reap."* This verse is feared by most people and viewed as a harsh warning. It sounds like God's going to get you for your wicked, immoral behavior. Paul is simply explaining the second law of the harvest. You reap what you sow, and you reap exactly what you sow! I never dreamed that the seeds that I had sown all those many years ago would be repaid in such a precious way.

Romans 8:28 is the first verse I ever taught my children. *"We know that to them that love God all things work together for good, even to them that are called according to his purpose."* This is a promise Satan can't do a thing about!

# Chapter 4

## Harvest Rule Three:
## You Reap Each and Every Time You Sow

*You may die twice or you may live twice, but you can't do both.*

It is now spring and Easter is around the corner. Dr. John Bisagno called me into his office and explained that there was a little church not far from my home. It was a mission church in need of a pastor. He asked if I would go preach there, survey the needs, and report back to him. Dr. John said he felt that the fellowship needed an evangelist. Dexter, one of the church elders, called and extended an invitation to me to preach on Easter Sunday.

The next thing I know, the church has invited me to become their new pastor. I accepted the call to become the pastor of Believers Baptist Church. After settling into a new ministry as a bi-vocational pastor, the church filled the baptismal. It was a baptismal which had experienced a prolonged drought. To my delight, the first person I ever baptized as the pastor of Believers Baptist Church was LeeAnn, my youngest child.

You cannot avoid reaping after you sow. You can only sow in the right direction or the wrong direction; you cannot do both. When you plant a seed it either grows healthily or unhealthily. In the rules of the harvest, it will ultimately grow even if it just lies dormant for years. Either way, you will pick the fruit of your labor when it is in season. Different things you plant will ripen in different seasons. You will always be dealing with the harvest of something from your past that you planted, either good or bad.

In Ecclesiastes 3, wise old Solomon writes that there is a time for everything.

*"There is an appointed time for everything. And there is a time for every event under heaven. A time to give birth and a time to die; A time to plant and a time to uproot what is planted. A time to kill and a time to heal; A time to tear down and a time to build up. A time to weep and a time to laugh; A time to mourn and a time to dance. A time to throw stones and a time to gather stones; A time to embrace and a time to shun embracing. A time to search and a time to give up as lost; A time to keep and a time to throw away. A time to tear apart and a time to sow together; A time to be silent and a time to speak. A time to love and a time to hate; A time for war and a time for peace."*

Birth and salvation are normal events for humans in the plan of God; whereas death and dying are abnormal. If you are a Christian, you go from life to life; only the unsaved move from death to death. You are born physically alive but Spiritually dead. You will stay dead unless your sprit is resurrected or brought back to life. Just like Jesus came back to life, He brings you and I back to life Spiritually. So when you physically die, you move from life on earth to life in heaven; thus Christians move from life to life. When you are born **Spiritually** dead and you physically die without ever accepting Jesus Christ as your Lord and Savior, you will move to eternal death; thus you move from death to death.

The Book of Jonah in the Old Testament provides a wonderful, living, contemporary example of the fact that you reap each and every time you sow. Have you ever asked, "What is God's will for my life?" Even the human with the darkest soul asks the meaning of life. In the story of Jonah, you will see a vivid picture of God's will in action. Two stories in the Old Testament, Noah's Ark and Jonah and the Whale are worldwide and universally known. Every souvenir shop, curio emporium, toy store, and glass menagerie store has Noah's Ark and Jonah in the belly of the whale. A buddhist wood carver in the local mall kiosk had a large inventory of

Jonah and the Whale's and Noah's Ark with animals. I asked him to tell me the story behind the ark. The vendor began the story of the flood with "the lord buddha sent a flood." This gave me the opportunity to share the real account from the Bible of Noah and Jonah. Upon my return to the mall, the wood carver had added a carving of a praying Noah on the deck of the ark and praying Jonah with the Whale.

Dr. Bisagno shares a story from his book, *The Power of Positive Prayer.* "An old missionary returned to the home of a convert among the Mohave Indians. When the missionary asked him how he was doing, old Joe said, 'Well it seems I have a black dog and a white dog inside of me and they are always fighting.' The missionary asked him, 'Which one wins?' Joe said, 'The one I feed that day.'"

To some people the Apostle Paul sounds like a schizophrenic because of what he writes in Romans 17: 15-17. Paul was simply addressing the issue of his personal struggle, experienced by all Christians, between the black and the white dog. Paul writes:

*"...what I am doing, I do not understand; for I am not practicing what I would like to do, but I am doing the very thing I hate. If I do the very thing I do not want to do, I agree with the Law, confessing that the Law is good. So now, no longer am I the one doing it, but sin which dwells in me."*

Jonah is having a black dog and white dog experience in his story. Jonah 1:1-3 tells of how Jonah flees from the Lord.

*"The word of the LORD came to Jonah son of Amittai: Go to the great city of Nineveh and preach against it, because its wickedness has come up before me. But Jonah ran away from the LORD and headed for Tarshish. He went down to Joppa, where he found a ship bound for that port. After paying the fare, he went aboard and sailed for Tarshish to flee from the LORD."*

The Bible says that the word of the Lord came to Jonah. Translated into 21st century language, God spoke to Jonah and he clearly understood the will of God for his life! God's plan, details, and direction were unmistakably spoken to Jonah. God's will for Jonah was to go to Nineveh and preach. This seems to be a very clear and straightforward task. All Jonah had to do was go and preach. The very next thing Jonah did was run away from God. He went the opposite direction of God's will. Nineveh was inland and Jonah ran into the sea. He turned tail and ran! Even though this is how it begins, the story will ultimately be about Jonah's success. The direction of success is waiting at the end of God's will. For a Christian, God's will and success are always in the same direction.

Oftentimes, Christians are confused. They want the blessing and they want the assurance of the blessing before they take any action. Individuals want a guarantee on their investment. Have you ever baked a cake that fell? Have you ever invested in a relationship that didn't work out? Do you have any money in the stock market or in a retirement fund where there is no guarantee? Christians want God's guarantee before they take action in His will. With God there is a guarantee! God guarantees blessings if you're in His will. To receive those blessings, you have to go in the direction of God's will. You're either going in the right direction or you're going in the wrong direction, but you can't do both.

Jonah is an excellent example of the fact that when God says, "Go," you must go in the direction He sends you. This is what I know about directions. No matter how far or how fast you travel in the wrong direction, you will never reach the right location. If you want to go to San Antonio, Texas, and you get on an airplane to China, you will not land in San Antonio. This is an absolute truth. You cannot travel in the wrong direction and get to the right place. Let's apply wrong directions to the other parts of life. You cannot spend your way out of debt. You cannot borrow your way out of debt. The only way to get out of debt is to work your way out of debt. At the end of that direction, blessings are waiting. You get out of debt by selling and making products to sell. I have never understood companies. The minute business starts faltering and sales go down, they lay off the salesmen. You can have the best widget in the world, but if no one knows about it, you will not sell one widget. The only way to be successful is to go in the right direction in each and every area of your life.

You can't be successful in life, family, business, or with your children by going in the wrong direction. But Jonah ran away from the Lord. There always seems to be the word BUT connected with any excuse or wrong direction in our life. Jonah knew he was going in the wrong direction, and he turned tail and ran, not walked, but ran as far as he could from the will of God. Each and every one of us has an excuse for not being in the will of God. We turn our backs on God and go the other direction. "But that little white lie didn't hurt anybody." "But if I report that, I'll have to pay it on income tax." "But what my wife doesn't know won't hurt her." There's always a BUT before the excuse for the wrong direction. You are either heading towards God's will and plan for your life or you're going in the wrong direction. You can't do both.

You can be a Christian and not be in the will of God. Jonah was a prophet. He was a preacher. He was a man of God. We don't know a great deal about Jonah except that he preached the single largest revival in the Old Testament. Jonah was obviously an anointed preacher, and he understood the will of God. It was his choice to go in the wrong direction. Sin is hard work. Look at all Jonah had to do to run away. First, he got a good workout when he ran all the way to Tarshish. Second, he had to find a boat and then dig deep into his broke, preacher pockets to pay the fare. So going the wrong direction cost Jonah in every way imaginable.

How do you know if you're out of God's will? You planned to be out of God's will! We don't accidentally slip out of the will of God. Each and every one of us knows the basics of God's will for our life. God directs us to specific people, places, and actions. These things are where God's blessings await us. Yet, we insist in going the wrong direction because of some insignificant inconvenience or some self-indulgent desire.

Christians have only two types of relationships with God. Be very clear that these relationships only pertain to Christians and not to people who do not have a personal relationship with the Lord Jesus Christ. The two types of relationships with God are the "china doll" relationship or the "rag doll" relationship. When you were a child, were you ever given a gift like a china doll or model boat or a very special collectible toy? You know, the kind of toy that you looked at but never played with; the toy that came with a warning. "Play with this very carefully. Keep it safe and it will be valuable someday. Place it on a shelf and protect it. It's precious and it is to be looked at and never held." So you placed the toy on the shelf and only took it down at special occasions just to show it off, and even then you were supervised.

Now the other toy, the one you loved and played with, is the rag doll. It could have been a blanket or stuffed animal or even a Kung Fu action grip G.I. Joe, but it was the toy you took with you everywhere. Everyone knew that it was your toy, even the other children. When it came time to play with toys, that's the one you brought to play time. Its hair was pulled off and it was dark gray from being dragged around the house. It's rag doll eyes had fallen out and had been stitched up many times by a loving mother. But at the same time, the loving mother was embarrassed to death by the pathetic looking toy. This very toy, which was mostly held together by dirt and love, was the toy with which you had a very special relationship.

This rag doll relationship brought you such joy, safety, and comfort when nothing else could. Christians who have china doll relationships with God have special occasion only relationships. Rag doll relationships are all of the time relationships. The rag doll relationship with God is the tougher of the two relationships because it is dragged through the mud, through the good days and bad days, for richer or poorer, in sickness and in health. When you lose contact with that relationship, it is just like losing your rag doll toy. You can't sleep until you find the rag doll. You work hard at reuniting the rag doll relationship. You do whatever it takes to find that toy again, just like when you were a child.

I have seen parents make the long trip back to the church or the daycare just to retrieve a toy from the nursery. The child would not go to sleep without that beloved toy. However, the child will sleep just fine with or without that expensive china doll. The child has an on-the-shelf relationship with the china doll. All too many professing Christians have a "keep God on-the-shelf except for special occasions" relationship. The reality is that the child doesn't care if the china doll is on the shelf or not. In the 21st century, many Christians find God just too inconvenient. God just doesn't seem to fit into their day planner.

I want to have a rag doll relationship with God. I want to lie down at night with Jesus' gentle, kind, reassuring arms around me. I want to wake up in the morning with the Holy Spirit's brilliant power illuminating my day. When I'm in the mud and sinking deep, I want to hang onto the hand of my Lord and be raised out of that place by the hand of Jesus. I want to take every step with Jesus. When my rag doll relationship is lost, I need to panic. In fact, it is the only time I need to panic. This self-imposed panic comes from my sin which has dislocated my relationship with Jesus. I immediately want my relationship with God back in place. I want my joy-filled, comfortable, rag doll relationship right at any cost. I want the daily walk with God. I don't care about the special occasion relationships: Christmas, Easter, baptisms, christening, weddings, and funerals. Don't get me wrong, during those occasions we need God because the events are important. These occasions are wonderful times of the year and are events in our lives we should celebrate together. But if your only involvement with God was when you attended the last wedding or the once-a-year Christmas or Easter church service, then you have a china doll relationship with Jesus.

You have two places in God's will. You can have the woodshed will relationship experience or have a perfect will relationship with God. Either way, as a Christian you will ultimately serve the will of God. Your children can be disobedient and go to the woodshed for correction and then go in the right direction, or your children can be obedient the first time and have blessings and praise heaped down upon them. When you do what you are supposed to do, good things happen. When your children do their homework and study, they make good grades. When the teenager cleans his room and does his chores, he gets to go out on Saturday night. When the student goes to school on time, he doesn't get detention. You get the blessings of an education without consequences.

In God's will, you do not have to think about what is right; you simply choose to do what is right. God declares that He will pour out blessings on you when you follow His will. Right is already set-up in the kingdom of God. The path is clear, the direction is plain, and God made it simple to follow His will. Sin complicates and convolutes the matter. God's will is just like school. The calendar is fixed, you arrive to school on time, you go to class, you sit in your assigned seat, and you receive an education. Every child has the same bell schedule and the same calendar, only the classes and teachers differ. Each child has a choice: to be on time or tardy, to do homework or receive a zero, to study hard and pass or to not study and fail. God's will is designed for our success. God's will is exclusively designed for the human race and the human race alone.

Jonah 1:17 says, *"And the LORD appointed a great fish to swallow Jonah, and Jonah was in the stomach of the fish three days and three nights."* Jonah, in the fish's belly, was having a woodshed experience. The message is simple. When you are out of God's will, you are in the wrong place. From Jonah's perspective, the belly of that fish was about as wrong as it gets. Christians must understand that my woodshed experiences and your woodshed experiences may be completely different. I can't get a DUI while driving because I don't drink. However, I can still get a speeding ticket because on occasion I have fractured the speed limit. We have consequences to our actions when our actions are out of God's will. Remember, you can't go in the right direction and the wrong direction at the same time. At the end of the right direction, there are blessings, and at the end of the wrong direction, there is a woodshed experience.

## Harvest Rule Three: You Reap Each and Every Time You Sow

Jesus said in Mark 3:25, *"If a house is divided against itself, that house will not be able to stand."* You cannot go in both directions at the same time!

# Chapter 5

## Fertilize Before the Harvest

*Remember, when you think your world is coming to the end,*
*it is already tomorrow in Australia.*
### Charles M. Schulz, Peanuts

I have never been in a fish's belly, but I have smelled them and cleaned them, and that's bad enough! Most people do not want the woodshed experience. I did not have to run many wind sprints to understand that I needed to be on time for practice. I did not have to get many speeding tickets to understand that I had a heavy foot. It took the principal only one or two swats for me to understand that bad behavior will not be tolerated in school. Most of us learn some of life's basics in the woodshed! Experience teaches us that bad behavior plainly costs time, energy, and money.

Now that Jonah was in about the worst position he could be in, what was his next step? He could have tried to swim his way out, claw his way out, or dig his way out, but instead he did what he should have done in the first place. Jonah prayed! Being a man of God, Jonah knew what to do! Jonah 2:1 says, *"From inside the fish Jonah prayed to the LORD his God."* He was kicked off the boat, swallowed by a fish, and then he began to pray. I love the way he started his prayer. Jonah prayed: *"In my distress I called to the LORD, and He (GOD) answered me. From the depths of the grave I called for help, and You listened to my cry."*

No matter how big a heathen you are, no matter how much you hate God, no matter how far away or how distant your relationship is with God, when it comes to a life or death situation, you will find the time and the words to pray. When you are faced with that emergency call of life or death, it makes no difference to you how foul your mouth is, how bad your attitude, or how deeply immersed in sin you are. You will begin to beg and bargain with God. When you are in the very cross hairs of death, and the crucible of the web of darkness lurches closer, your cries become more desperate. The husband who receives a call at midnight; the mother with the missing child; the passenger in the out of control car; the successful businessman with the x-rays showing the long undetected tumor; or the soldier in the fox hole; all know Jonah's prayer.

It's hard to find comfort in that midnight hour as your stomach keeps score and sleep escapes you while you walk the floor trying to talk to God. If you have a china doll relationship, then like china, it is a fragile relationship. The distant and dusty relationship with the china doll is hard and cold. Give me the old comfortable, huggable, rag doll faith to wrap my arms around and love. These are some words of the classic hymn of a reformed slave trader, "Amazing Grace, how sweet the sound…..T'was Grace that taught my heart to fear…..'Tis Grace that brought us safe thus far and Grace will lead us home." Grace is the name of the rag doll in your relationship with Jesus.

You know where the arms of Jesus are and you know where to fall because you have the absolute trust He will catch you in that darkest hour. You have such a relationship with the rag doll that all you have to do is pull it close to you and cry. Your relationship needs no formal *"Hallowed be thy name."* You just need to reach out to the loving, tender arms of your Father who is awaiting your tears as an offering. It is not just the consistent availability of the Father, but it is also each of us having a relationship of trust with our great Savior and King.

Jonah 1:17 tells us, *"But the LORD provided a great fish to swallow Jonah, and Jonah was inside the fish three days and three nights."* So Jonah prayed while he was in the woodshed. He was like that Toyota commercial from years ago, "You asked for it, you got it, Toyota."

In Jonah's case, he got a woodshed experience with God. You reap what you sow (You got it!). You reap exactly what you sow, and you reap each and every time you sow. Boy, oh boy, is Jonah reaping it now! Now Jonah gets it and begins to pray. This is the only recorded prayer by Jonah, but he was in the belly of the fish for three days. I want to assure you that this was not his only prayer. Jonah did not cease from praying. Jonah 2:10 says, *"And the LORD commanded the fish, and it vomited Jonah onto dry land."* Jonah was still praying when that fish began to vomit because he had no idea where the fish was going to vomit him. He could have been at the bottom of the sea. Yes, things could get worse. Jonah was praying all the way *in* that fish, and he was praying all the way *out*! God was merciful, and the fish vomited him on to the beach.

Jonah 3: 1-2 states, *"'Now the word of the LORD came to Jonah the second time, saying, 'Arise, go to Nineveh the great city and proclaim to it the proclamation which I am going to tell you.'"* Let's review the first time Jonah received the word of the Lord. God said, "Go preach to Nineveh." Jonah said, "NO!" Then Jonah went the wrong direction. Next, Jonah went to the holy woodshed, "the belly of the fish," and was vomited onto the shore. God spoke to Jonah once more and said, "Go Preach to Nineveh." What changed? Jonah decided to go in God's direction. God's will for your life does not change. God did not change, the message did not change, the need did not change, and God's messenger did not change. The only thing that changed was Jonah's direction.

What you are sowing needs to change if you want to reap a new crop. Jonah missed the blessings he could have received without the "belly of the fish" experience. Jonah did not have to go to the woodshed to get blessed! If your life is going in the wrong direction, then you are missing the blessings that God has waiting for you at the end of the right direction. The ultimate blessing is at the end of God's will. Time keeps going. The farther you travel from God's good direction for your life, the more time passes and the farther you are from God's ultimate blessings. I do not know what beach Jonah was vomited onto, but I suspect he was even farther from Nineveh than when he started. The fact is, time will go on with or without God's will, direction, and blessing in your life. It is God's great gift to include you in His will. If you desire an interesting study, read the full text of Jonah's prayer. Each and every word of Jonah's prayer testifies that he knew he should go in the right direction.

For Jonah, one time in the fish was enough. Yet, there are plenty of people who have to keep going back to the woodshed over and over again. Relationship after relationship, multiple divorces, rehabilitation over and over again, credit card debt, DUI's; the list is endless. You cannot go in the wrong direction and end up in the right place! You can go in your direction or you can go in God's direction. **Do not count toys and dollars in the bank as your ultimate success! God doesn't!**

*A great man of faith, Booker T. Washington, said, "Success is to be measured not so much by the position that one has reached in life as by the obstacles which he has overcome."*

God only measures success by His will, not by what man thinks about God. I read a bumper sticker after I had first accepted Jesus Christ as my Lord and Savior many years ago. The bumper sticker said, "God said it, I believe it, and that settles it." On the surface, that boot strap theology sounds good. But the reality is that what I believe or what I do not believe makes no difference at all! All things are settled by God's Word, not my belief.

The legend goes, many years ago, the University of Chicago Divinity School would have an annual day they called "Baptist Day." On this day, each person was to bring a lunch to be eaten outdoors in a grassy picnic area. The school would invite one of the greatest modern minds to lecture in the theological education hall on every Baptist Day.

The following story illustrates man's knowledge versus the raw reality of God. One year, Dr. Paul Tillich was invited to lecture. Dr.

Tillich spoke for two and one-half hours, proving that the resurrection of Jesus was false. He quoted scholar after scholar and book after book. He concluded that since there was no such thing as the historical resurrection, then the religious tradition of the church was groundless, emotional mumbo-jumbo because it was based on a relationship with a risen Jesus, who in fact, never rose from the dead in any literal sense.

He then asked if there were any questions. After about 30 seconds, an old, dark skinned preacher with a head of short-cropped, woolly white hair stood up in the back of the auditorium. "Docta Tillich, I got one question," he said as all eyes turned toward him. He reached into his sack lunch and pulled out an apple and began eating it. "Docta Tillich...CRUNCH, MUNCH...My question is a simple question...CRUNCH, MUNCH...Now, I ain't never read them books you read...CRUNCH, MUNCH...and I can't recite the Scriptures in the original Greek. I don't know nothin' about Niebuhr and Heidegger...CRUNCH, MUNCH." He finished the apple. "All I wanna know is: this apple I just ate - was it bitter or sweet?"

Dr. Tillich paused for a moment and answered in exemplary scholarly fashion, "I cannot possibly answer that question, for I haven't tasted your apple." The white-haired preacher dropped the core of his apple into his crumpled paper bag, looked up at Dr. Tillich, and calmly said, "Neither have you tasted my Jesus" The 1,000 plus in attendance could not contain themselves. The auditorium erupted with applause and cheers. Dr. Tillich thanked his audience and promptly left the platform.

# Chapter 6

## All Fruit Does Not Ripen at the Same Time

*When you are traveling in the wrong direction, no matter how far you travel, you never end up in the right place. You are either in God's will or you're out of God's will; you can't be in both places at the same time.*

Jonah, now out of the fish and on the beach, is traveling in the right direction with the same instruction to go preach to the people of Nineveh. We're told in Jonah 3:3 - 4 that,

*Jonah arose and went to Nineveh according to the word of the LORD. Now Nineveh was an exceedingly great city, a three days' walk. Then Jonah began to go through the city one day's walk; and he cried out and said, "Yet forty days and Nineveh will be overthrown."*

Wow, what a message. The people of Nineveh must have loved hearing they were all doomed. Jonah was a foreigner and a Hebrew, one of their most despised enemies. He came proclaiming their total annihilation and demise! Jonah told them that the pagan gods they worshiped were wrong and could not save them. The only chance to save their lives was to switch and worship the God of their enemies, the Jews. What was even more amazing was that the people of Nineveh did not just simply kill this Hebrew troublemaker. Jonah had no compassion on the people when he delivered his message. He hated the people and they were his enemies. To Jonah, the people of Nineveh were an unclean, idolatrous people who deserved God's judgment. Finally, the most astonishing thing happened. Jonah 3:5 tells us, *"Then the people of Nineveh believed in God; and they called a fast and put on sackcloth from the greatest to the least of them."* The people of Nineveh listened to the word of God.

Success always begins with one individual repenting. The individual must turn around and go in the right direction. The process of success began with Jonah. His success expanded to the people of Nineveh. When the people of a nation turn back to God, the leaders will turn to God. Sinners vote for sinners and Christians vote for Christians. Jonah 3:6 - 11 says,

> *"When the word reached the king of Nineveh, he arose from his throne, laid aside his robe from him, covered himself with sackcloth and sat on the ashes. "He issued a proclamation and it said, In Nineveh by the decree of the king and his nobles: Do not let man, beast, herd, or flock taste a thing. Do not let them eat or drink water. "But both man and beast must be covered with sackcloth; and let men call on God earnestly that each may turn from his wicked way and from the violence which is in his hands. "Who knows, God may turn and relent and withdraw His burning anger so that we will not perish. "When God saw their deeds, that they turned from their wicked way, then God relented concerning the calamity which He had declared He would bring upon them. And He did not do it. 'Should I not have compassion on Nineveh, the great city in which there are more than 120,000 persons who do not know the difference between their right and left hand, as well as many animals?'"*

Let's do a little math. There were 120,000 men with an estimated 2.5 children per man with wives. In addition, this was a culture of polygamy, so each man probably had many wives and concubines. Nineveh was home to a large slave population from their many conquests. Taking all this into consideration, a conservative population estimate would be about 800,000 people. To feed this large a number of people, it would take roughly 2,000,000 head of livestock per year. God's man Jonah goes the wrong direction and ends up in the woodshed. God's man prays and then goes in the right direction. Jonah preaches to a kingdom of heathens. His message is not "Jesus loves me this I know," but a message of "You are going to die painfully in 40 days." The people of Nineveh did not have a hand-holding, hugging relationship with Jonah, but a hellfire, repenting relationship full of judgment.

This is a great sidebar lesson for the nation. When the Spiritual leader gets right with God, then the individual called by God repents and preaches the word of God to the people of the nation. From the least to the greatest, the people of the nation repent and get right with God. Then when the people of a nation repent, it leads to national repentance. This will in turn lead to a national revival.

The people of Nineveh became very serious about individual prayer. They did not eat or drink. The people of Nineveh were fasting and praying while dressed in sackcloth. In the Old Testament, sackcloth is what the prophets would wear to preach, "Repent, fast, mourn, weep and pray because God is going to judge you and our nations." The people were judging themselves before God could. By the time the news reached the king of Nineveh, the nation was already in revival. Then the king caught on and said, "Wow, we need everybody to get involved, including all the livestock." The people did not wait on the king to get right with God; the folks, from the least to the greatest, led the revival.

National revival always leads to the election of leaders who are doing God's will. When God's will becomes the will of the people, then God will bless the nation. This is our country's problem in a nutshell. So if you do not like the elected officials, then you need to repent! If you are waiting on those weak willed people in Washington to lead our country into the next greater awakening, you are in for a dry spell. Success always begins with individual repentance. It will become such a Spiritual expectation that the leaders won't be able to resist the irresistible grace of the Lord Jesus Christ. II

Chronicles 7:13 - 15 states,

*"If I shut up the heavens so that there is no rain, or if I command the locust to devour the land, or if I send pestilence among My people, and My people who are called by My name humble themselves and pray and seek My face and turn from their wicked ways, then I will hear from heaven, will forgive their sin and will heal their land. Now My eyes will be open and My ears attentive to the prayer offered in this place."*

This is powerful, and it is just as real today!

The reality is that you will always reap more than you sow. This is an absolute law of the harvest. If you plant one bean seed, the bean plant will produce many beans from that one seed. The Spiritual power of revival always begins with one man committed to the direction of God's will. God sent Jonah (one man) to lead the greatest revival in the Old Testament, and Jonah did it without backyard Bible clubs, vacation Bible school, buildings, budgets, the internet, or Bibles. Jonah's message was doom and gloom, but it was accomplished through the power of God. Jonah's straightforward commitment to doing God's will led to his success.

Ultimate success always waits for you when you are in God's will. This one guy, in some old, smelly fish clothes which were probably bleached white from the fish's stomach acid, led a bunch of idol worshiping, pagan people to repentance. What could the Living God of the universe do with you? If I had been Jonah when I got out of that fish, I would have run all the way to Nineveh in fear of what might eat me next. Whatever fish's belly or wrong direction you are in today, remember that the right direction always begins with prayer. Prayer is the device God has chosen to communicate with you. This communication is impossible unless the right number is dialed. To talk to the Father, it must go through the mediator Jesus Christ. Acts 4:12 tells us, *"And there is salvation in no one else; for there is no other name under heaven that has been given among men by which we must be saved."*

# Chapter 7

## Harvest Rule Four:
## You Reap Later Than You Sow

*Impossible is just a big word thrown around by small men who are supported by smaller minded men.*

Small minded men find it easier to live in the world than to change the world. If you say something loud enough and long enough, you become what you profess. The word *impossible* is no more than a declaration of opinion which needs the smallness of man to sustain it. Wherever small minded people gather, there are even smaller minded people supporting them.

It was the beginning of the eighth grade when I knelt by my bedside and sincerely prayed for the first time. I still remember the essence of my prayer. I said, "God, they say you are the Father in heaven, and, well, I need a father on earth. So you will have to do both jobs. I do not understand who Jesus is, but I will take Him as Lord. I do not know what that means! I just know that I need you right now." From that moment forward, I was a Christian. I did not even fully realize it, but my life began to change. This prayer from my childhood was uttered after one of my father's typical alcoholic rages. My earthly father had failed on many levels. He was a hardened alcoholic, and my mother was a Jedi black belt codependent, so she was not much help.

My father had grown up during the 1930's in the middle of the depression. He lived the type of life made for a TV mini-series. By the age of 14, he had been to Europe twice as a cabin boy, trying to keep food on the table for his mother, brothers, and sisters back in Texas. Near the end of the depression, my father, his oldest brother, and a friend dug telephone post holes across the country in the government work program. The 10 foot long, handheld post hole diggers cut through solid rock across America. This built muscle upon muscle in their bodies.

They found themselves in Alaska before it was a state in the Union. In all their pictures, they are dressed like wooly cowboys with their Colt 45 revolvers slung on their hips. They staked a claim for a gold mine in Nome, Alaska. During the darkest part of winter, they left the mine to live with their friend, the territorial governor, in Fairbanks.

The governor had been elected because he owned the only bar in town. When they returned to Nome, they found their equipment and the remains of their gold mine buried under fifty feet of ice and snow from an avalanche. They returned to Fairbanks and purchased a business. Their business was a single engine, open cockpit airplane. It looked like the Spirit of St. Louis that Charles Lindberg flew; only this one was held together by duct tape and snow skis. The plane came with two flying lessons: how to get up and how to get down. My dad's brother Jim became the pilot, and they started the first airmail service from Alaska to Canada. Within a year, they were able to sell the business and drive back to Texas.

World War II was on the horizon and there was a lack of employment options for my father because of his eighth grade education. He ultimately joined the U.S. Marines Corps. With his large physique and his case-hardened toughness, he quickly advanced in rank. He became a Sergeant and a Drill Instructor. With the eruption of WWII, he was called to action. My father had crystal blue eyes, jet black hair, and a Schwarzenegger body. He was honored to have his picture placed on a recruiting poster for the U.S. Marines. My dad should have gone to Hollywood.

My father would serve with distinction in the island hopping campaign of the South Pacific. He, like so many other veterans of war, would come out of the jungles decorated and wounded, with malaria and the early stages of alcoholism. These events would cause decomposition and decay in the balance of his life. The hardships that forged his life would have broken many men. My father was filled with pessimism and anger. His lack of education crumbled his self-esteem. To be brilliant and have limited options in an educated world hardened his heart. The hardness of his heart made anger spew from his mouth like an erupting volcano. He was a raging alcoholic fortified by booze.

As a very young child, I once asked him if he killed anyone during the war, and he said, "You go into battle feeling one way, and you come out feeling different forever." The combination of low self-esteem and guilt facilitated an authentic hate for God and all things Christian or religious. Christmas was nothing but a reason to drink more and stay drunk. The only Christmas I remember enjoying as a child was the year it fell on Sunday and the liquor stores were closed. For my dad, it was easier to abandon God because he felt that God had abandoned him. We always criticize the things we hate the most, and boy did he let God have a piece of his mind. Sergeant Barnette also personally invented and perfected profanity. As a Drill Instructor, he had a finely honed vocabulary of superlatives. The other DI's said that he could make them blush. It is no easy feat to make a Marine DI blush. His words were like rubbing alcohol and sandpaper on your bare skin. The words rubbed so many sore spots that after awhile you became numb.

In the eighth grade, I announced my newfound faith in Jesus Christ to my family. My father began his systematic demeaning and dismantling of my faith. My father's mocking comments were surgical in their strikes. With Marine Corps efficiency, he had every opportunity to reduce my young faith to rubble. In reality, I think he was glad I had something to believe in other than booze. He would say things like, "Tom, we need to get you a big tent and a bunch of one armed deacons, so when you preach they can't steal from the offering bucket." The year went by, and it was my freshman summer in high school when my father became very ill.

The two packs of Camel cigarettes and the fifth of Canadian Club each and every day of his life finally damaged his health beyond repair. My father had multiple massive surgeries. My family, which still had some interest in his repulsive life, had gathered outside his ICU room out of family obligation. Instead of an atmosphere of prayer and hope for his life, it was a countdown to his death. Hell and heaven were not of any interest to my relatives or the state of my father's eternal soul. The somber mood reminded me of the words written on the gates of hell in Dante's Divine Comedy, *"Abandon hope all ye who enter here."* All hope had been abandoned. My dad's next stop would be the fires of hell. His death would come as a relief because it would end his pain and the pain he caused others. Those who knew him best were also convinced that he would or could never change, even if he survived. If death ever had an optimistic crowd, it was my family.

Have you ever considered who would stand outside your ICU room door when it's your turn and the countdown starts? Even more important, what would the people outside the door say about your life? My father had been asking for me by name. Dad always called me "baby." I went into my dad's ICU room alone. I was 15 years old, and was only a one year old Christian. I had never seen an ICU room, and it was quite a shock at age 15. Lying helplessly before me was the most ferocious and angry person I had ever known. My father was now shriveled, weak, and dying. He was conscious and alert. The doctors could not give him anything for the pain because he would not wakeup. I took his hand and drew close to him.

My words cannot adequately describe the feelings and events that followed. In that moment, I would be bolder than I had ever been. It was the kind of supernatural boldness that comes from being gripped by the Holy Spirit, who will not let you go until the sea is parted. This was not emotion but real courage. Courage and bravery come from faith, never emotion. Courage through faith is the experienced reality of God. The result of this courage will be demonstrated through your actions, never your feelings. Great feelings will always follow great faith. Faith is not, and will never be produced by emotions. Real courage is a pure act of unselfishness, regardless of the consequence. My initial five minute visit with my father turned into hours. The wise and kind attending nurse instinctively knew the seriousness of my business. I suspect she had seen the closing moments of life many times in her career. The business I was conducting with my father and the outcome of it held eternal consequences.

My father would become the very first person I ever had the privilege of sharing God's plan of salvation with. I had the privilege of leading him to the saving knowledge of the Lord, Jesus Christ. My earthly father now had a heavenly Father. I had no Bible, and we did not speak of religion or theology. I only had one simple question as I held out both hands. I said, "In this hand I have heaven and in this hand I have hell. Where do you wish to go when you die?" My dad chose heaven. The next step was to simply lead him through the process of becoming a new child in God. The Apostle Paul writes the simple plan of salvation in Romans 10:9 - 10, *"If you confess with your mouth, 'Jesus is Lord,' and believe in your heart that God raised Him from the dead, you will be saved. With the heart one believes, resulting in righteousness, and with the mouth one confesses, resulting in salvation."*

What a gift God gave me. Impossible was the typical word family and friends would use to describe my father. There was no way he would ever get sober; no way he could ever change. My dad would have been voted the man least likely to become a Christian. Yet before my eyes, my father became a Christian. He never drank or even touched another drop of booze! My dad would beat the countdown to death that night. He would live for two more years, mostly in the hospital. Dad had regular Bible studies with men from the Gideon Bible Society in the Veterans Hospital until his death. I do not know the names of these men, but I will be forever thankful. The most significant words my dad ever spoke to me before his death was, "I wish I had known Him (Jesus) all my life."

In the hospital that night, waves of realization came over me. I am pleased to say the boldness that gripped me that night has never let go. I have let go of God at times, but not the power of the Holy Spirit. As I type these words, I have tears running down my face. The great news is that I will see my father again, and that together we will worship the Lord Jesus.

The other remarkable realization that would change me forever was the Spiritual understanding that if I could lead my dad (who I considered the scariest man on earth) to Jesus Christ, then this Jesus stuff had real power. At that point, I began to move forward with the understanding of the power available to me on earth. I learned that I could wield the Word of God and the name of Jesus like a sword. I also came to the realization that compared to the terror of sharing the gospel with my dad, sharing with other people was not frightening at all. I think that must have been the way Peter felt after walking on the water into Jesus' arms. Emboldened is the word I have frequently used to describe my experience.

Satan had control of my father throughout all those years of alcohol and anger. His life was taken back that night in the hospital. Satan no longer had a claim on him. The devil lost! I am also pleased to say that the cost to Satan has been 1000's of souls. Over my years in ministry, I have had the privilege of sharing the gospel and leading 1000's of people to call upon the name of the Lord, Jesus Christ as their Savior.

Satan paid a high price for the pain in my father's life. As a counselor, each time I am privileged to help an alcoholic recover or a family heal or a teenager get off drugs, I reclaim a small part of my dad's life. I have reaped time and time again from the crop that I sowed that night in my dad's hospital room. It's an example of how some crops that we sow are never ending.

## The Rule of 52's Five Harvest Laws of Sowing and Reaping (Planting and Picking)

1. You reap what you sow
2. You reap exactly what you sow
3. You reap each and every time you sow
4. You reap more than you sow
5. You reap later than you sow

The dictionary provides a simple definition of permanency (root word *permanent*): "Not expected to change for an indefinite time; not temporary; an enduring condition that cannot change." Permanency is both an element and an end result of the five laws of the harvest. It is part of the rules of sowing and reaping. The impossible things become possible only when the scars of life are turned over to the Father. To paraphrase Genesis 50:20, *"Satan planned evil against me; God planned it for good to bring about the present result of the survival of many people."* God has a plan, and the results of God's plan will always be good. God's plan will always bring permanent success. Restoration is also part of the law of the harvest. I gleaned a harvest from my dad, Sergeant Robert Barnette, USMC: father, husband, alcoholic, born again Christian, and servant of his Lord, Jesus Christ.

Thomas Payne wrote:

*"The harder the conflict, the more glorious the triumph. What we obtain too cheaply, we esteem too lightly; it is dearness only that gives everything its value. I love the man that can smile in trouble and who can gather strength from distress and grow brave by reflection. 'Tis the business of little minds to shrink; but he whose heart is firm, and whose conscience approves his conduct, will pursue his principles unto death."*

## Whose Woods Are These?

*Sometimes inspiration finds you even when you do not want to be bothered by it.*

As a college freshman, I learned two things. The first thing was that my momma was not there to wash my clothes. Number two: college was not high school. This is a revelation that all first time college students must experience. During my first year, less than sterling academic performance landed me in summer school. I had been recruited by a major college in my sport, which was the good news. The bad news was that in order to transfer to the new school, I needed to jumpstart my GPA.

As a result of this experience, I added a new slang term to my vocabulary, "Sco Pro", which is short for scholastic probation. I attended summer school at Houston Baptist University and took what I perceived to be easy courses, one of which was Speech 101. I walked into a small upstairs classroom with 13 other students who had also recently become familiar with the term Sco-pro. The other students were there for precisely the same reason; it was an effortless class which would inflate their GPA.

The summer school students walked into the classroom one by one and took a seat. We were all a little stunned to see the professor seated on top of his desk in a standard teacher's chair. It was certainly not something you see every day at a major university. The class was silent and frozen; the only sound was the hum of the air conditioner. The professor introduced himself and told the class to get out a piece of paper and write our name, date, and heading because we were about to take a test. The professor said, "The University requires all students to take a written test, so number your paper one through twenty." He gave us a simple spelling test which I am sure I failed.

Then the professor announced, "This is speech class, so we are going to speak. That was your one and only written test." He opened a book on his lap and read out loud the following words from *Stopping by Woods on a Snowy Evening*, "Whose woods these are I think I know. His house is in the village though; He will not see me stopping here." When he finished the poem, we stared at him with the mostly unimpressed, blank stares of disinterested summer school students. Our obvious indifference did not discourage the professor. He explained that Robert Frost was the author of the poem and that he was one of the most celebrated American poets. The professor further explained that Robert Frost had written many poems in the midst of suffering and personal tragedy. This anguish would influence most of Frost's written works. The devastating losses in his life included the untimely death of his sister, two of his children, and his wife. He knew the soul's depths of dejection, and he had promised his wife upon her death to keep writing. "He had miles to go before he could sleep."

Our professor read the poem again and told us to listen for the meaning. Upon the second reading of the poem, the class engaged in a lively philosophical debate of possible meanings. The professor sat silently while our elementary debate and attempt at analysis of the written word seized our minds.

The professor took charge of discussion once again, and the class listened intently. He began by explaining that he had attended the University of Michigan in Ann Arbor, and that his professor had been Robert Frost, the author of the poem. The professor described his classroom experience with Professor Robert Frost. The students would sit on the classroom floor around Frost as he sat in an overstuffed lounge chair and talked. Sometimes Frost would read poems, and sometimes they would write. Our professor paused in his storytelling to share a very powerful thought. It was one of those ideas that never left my thoughts. He told us that because he had learned at the feet of the master of American poetry, Robert Frost, my professor was now the first generation transference of knowledge and truth. That meant our class would now become a second generation conveyance of knowledge and truth, but only if we had the power to pick up the gauntlet which he tossed before our class. That makes you, the reader of this story, the third generation reader or knowledge and truth.

You probably could have seen the brain dead part of my mind grow 10 sizes that day. Up until that point in my life, reading was something which was mandatory and assigned by teachers. It was torturously applied only as needed and as a last resort. I rarely read anything other than comic books, newspaper cartoons, price tags, and of course the Bible.

But all that changed in an instant. I was intrigued by the Robert Frost story, and I wanted to know more. I slipped into the library on campus after class, checked out several books by and about Robert Frost, took the books home, and devoured them. This was before the time of backpacks, so I hid the books behind the seat of my truck. I did not want any of my jock/redneck drinking buddies finding out I was a closet poetry reader.

For the rest of the summer semester my classmates and I would meet before and after class to read and discuss the merits of our new found love of poetry. Today I own thousands of books in my personal library that I have collected over a lifetime of literary exploration. I owe a great debt to my professor. He was a dear man of God who has gone home to be with the Lord.

## Please Take the Following Test

Pretend you are given $200 million dollars in cash. It's free and it's yours! All you have to do to earn the money is unlearn your primary language; English, German, or whatever language you acquired as a child.

Your language is one of the primary survival skills you learned to meet your needs. You learned to ask for what you need. Later you learned to verbalize what you wanted. First you asked for a cookie, later you wanted a chocolate chip cookie.

Now to acquire the $200 million dollars, you can take as much time as you would like. You may educate yourself in any form or fashion desired. You can immerse yourself in a new language and culture. But at the end of the day, you must eradicate (totally forget) your original primary language, not just learn a new language. Do you think this is possible? The answer is NO! The permanent footprint of your primary language can never be erased. Each and every word you speak has meaning and motivation, which are absolute truths. When God spoke at the time of creation, He said that all He had created was good. The Father created by the Living Word.

Your words have the power to create and destroy. Word choice is based on life events, perceived needs, wants, and reality. Humans are immersed in either normal reality or abnormal reality, which shapes their basic wants. Words have meaning! Each word that is spoken has a specific meaning, which is exclusively based on perceived wants and real needs. Every time a person says, "Hi, how are you doing?" or, "Thank you," there is a motivation and thought behind the words. The speaking of each word is an attempt to have a need met.

Words do not originate from the mechanics of the ability to speak, they are learned. Each word you know was learned from another source. Learning words in a specific culture gives the words meaning. If words have meaning, then the use of the words have motivation. If all words have meaning and motivation, then they must have purpose. The five basic needs are the driving purpose. The reason we speak is because we have needs!

What determines your needs is your normal or abnormal reality. If a boy says, "I love you," to his mother, then the word love has motivation and specific emotional meaning. If a boy says, "I love you," to his dog, then his affection for the dog is clearly understood. "Love" takes on an entirely different meaning if the boy's mother dies or if the boy's dog dies. The depth of loss and remorse felt by the boy is significantly different. Same word, same feeling, but the mother met a very different set of basic needs in the boy's life. The dog also met a need in the boy's life, but the greater the need, the greater the effect on a persons reality. The loss of the mother affected the boy's reality more than the loss of the dog. Our words are the outer expression of our inner needs or wants.

I went back to visit Mrs. Mitchell, my second grade teacher, during my first year in college. I do not know what surprised her more, that I came back to visit or I was in college. The children in her class were all lining up for the bathroom when one little boy broke free from the herd and ran around the room yelling. I stood dumbfounded, waiting for Mrs. Mitchell to spring into action. The other children just stood in line and then proceeded out the door. The boy suddenly stopped and just sat down on the floor. She leaned over to me and asked, "What do you think little Johnny is trying to tell us?" I knew then why she was one of my favorite teachers. Little Jonny was speaking volumes; I just wasn't listening in his language.

Dr. Bisagno once asked a profound question to the church. Does a missionary in Africa try to teach the people English before he preaches the gospel? No, the missionary learns to speak the language of the people. The missionary communicates the gospel of the Bible in their language! To understand little Johnny I needed to understand what he was trying to communicate. He had some underlying need that was motivating his behavior. He was probably trying to express a need he did not know how to share. Examples could be, "I don't like bathroom because that is where I was sexually abused." Or it could be as simple as, "I am a second grader and I want to be in control. You can't tell me what to do."

All words must be considered in the context of the reality in which they are spoken. A woman in Africa who speaks Swahili will express love to her child in her language, and an English speaking mother in America will tell her child, "I love you." The emotion of the expression is universal. The need for love is universal; it's just the language that is different.

American soldiers held captive during the Vietnam War were not allowed to utilize the English language. All POWs had to learn Vietnamese if they wished to speak to each other or to their captors. The POWs would not receive any food, medical attention, or correspondence if they didn't speak Vietnamese. Words became a source of control for the captors and a source of survival for the POWs.

A number of prisoners were held for many years, yet upon their release and return to the United States, very few of the soldiers retained more than a 30 word vocabulary of the Vietnamese language. Many forgot the language altogether. Universally, all of the American POWs retained their original English language. This is an example of how it is impossible to extinguish reality skills once they are acquired. Language is a universal survival skill used by all people and societies.

The seed which the professor sowed in the minds of the 13 teenage college students that summer forever changed their lives. Words from my professor would forever change my life. "I have miles to go before I sleep and miles to go before I sleep."

## What Is The Greatest Motivator?

We each have 5 basic needs, and these needs dominate our words. Survival is the first need in the hierarchy of needs. Our words develop from these needs naturally. What do you think a starving child in Darfur talks about all day and night; their toys, sleepovers, or birthday parties? Of course not! They talk about food and how to get food. Their need to survive is motivated by pain, and pain shapes their words. Pain is the greatest universal motivator. All individuals resist pain because it is the greatest builder of individual walls.

The recoiling result of pain in life is the construction of a wall or prison around the mind, body, and Spirit. When the wall is held together with fear, hate, hurt, and especially unforgiveness, it becomes a self-generator of pain. The sad thing is that the wall really does not keep the pain out. The wall of pain is a closed system, like a rat cage. Pain, emotional waste, and abnormal reality are kept inside the walls.

The wall is a retaining partition that allows the bitterness and anger to rot and fester until it consumes you and others. Individuals are only let inside the wall of abnormality (pain) when they are willing to live the life of pain with you. Abnormal pain teaches children to build their own walls. They learn the words and language of pain from their parents, one abnormal brick at a time.

When an alcoholic stumbles home drunk, how often will the mother send the children to their rooms to hide to avoid the pain? She will tell them to be quiet and not upset daddy. She is hoping he will just pass out before he can inflict too much pain. Pain always teaches a vocabulary of abnormal terms.

Imagine a chain link fence around a yard. The fence lets things in and it lets things out. The fence provides some protection, but the protection is only real if others respect the fence. The fence in the yard also defines what a person owns. Chances are good that the toys, bikes, flowers, and lawnmower inside the fence belong to the person who owns the fence. A fence defines ownership or boundaries.

These boundaries can provide instructions such as, "play in your own yard, keep the dog in the fence, close the gate, or no trespassing." What would happen if the fence moves or changes shape every time the homeowner leaves his home? One day the fence is shaped like a diamond; the next day it is shaped like a right triangle; the next day a figure eight; and so on. The movable fence provides none of the benefits that a fence should!

The abnormal fence is a problem. The thing that keeps moving the fence is pain. First, the abnormal fence has no normal corner post. Next, the fence wants to be stable, but the pain keeps reshaping the fence. It's like when your back hurts and you can't find any comfortable position for sleep; you toss and turn because of the pain. Finally, nothing can function normally in the fenced area because the pain magic monkey is moving the fence.

One of the key elements to *The Rule of 52* and your success is accepting the concept of normal and abnormal reality. If something is causing pain in your life, then its source is abnormal. Your words will help you identify this abnormality. Ask yourself if the words you use convey the real meaning of what you are trying to say? An example of misdirected meaning is when you tell your husband, "You don't love me!" What you are really trying to say is, "I wish you would tell me you love me."

Jesus Christ, the Lord and Savior, knew how to be authentically free. He refused to build a wall in His life. He would not embrace darkness no matter how much it was forced upon Him. The darkness of hopelessness is bondage and a complete lack of freedom. Who in your life do you feel like you cannot forgive? Who in your life have you withdrawn from and consciously built a wall between? Who in your life do you go out of your way to avoid? Who do you constantly remind about his or her past sins? Who do you blame for thrusting abnormal reality upon you? Do you say things like, "I love you, but I just can't forgive you. I just can't trust you anymore"? All of these statements and ideas contain the prison of hopelessness.

If you cannot forgive the people of your past, then ask God to bless them. Jesus taught people how to overcome their pain of the past and start living in the present. Jesus teaches us how to start down the path of freedom from the past in Matthew 5: 44. He gives us the bless'em principle, saying, *"But I say unto you, love your enemies and bless those that curse you, do good to them that hate you, and pray for them which despitefully use you and persecute you."*

If you don't have the strength to ask God with a clear heart to forgive these individuals, then ask God to bless them. First ask God to forgive your unforgiveness. Then ask God to bless you, and your heart, and your actions. Next ask God to help you forgive those who have cursed you and who have thrust their abnormal reality upon you. Immerse yourself in asking God to prepare your heart to be blessed with an attitude of forgiveness.

Take a deep breath and do the unthinkable: ask God to bless the person or people who have hurt you, and be very specific. Ask God to bless them in all aspects of their lives in detail, even in the special areas where they cursed you. Finally, turn everything over to God, and ask Him to bless your motives, actions, and feelings. I have found that it is very difficult for me to hate someone and carry the pain of unforgiveness if I am asking God to bless them.

Many years ago when I was a youth minister, a young woman came into my church office. She pulled out a revolver and she said, "I know where my husband is and he is lying up with some woman. I am going to go shoot me two people this afternoon!"

I persuaded her to hand me the revolver and sit down. I shared with her that she had a greater responsibility to her three children. The immediate crisis was averted, and we continued to visit weekly! Over time the husband left and they were divorced.

Once again, the young woman came into my office in a crisis. She showed me a handful of loose change and said, "This money is the only thing left between me and starvation or prostitution." She was determined to care for her children at all cost. She said that her ex-husband had not paid child support in a number of months. Over a cup of coffee and a long conversation, I shared with her the principle of asking God to bless someone who had caused pain in life. The pain can be from the past, present, or future! In this case, the pain was in the past, present, *and* future. She was facing extreme hardship, and her hope was now fading fast. Spiritually she had prayed and given of her time and talent to God. She had sturdy faith in God, but she still felt hopeless. The pain of hunger was real.

It is critical to note that she was still a prisoner of her dysfunctional marriage and the abnormal reality it created. The pain from her past was destroying her hope in the present and for the future. I simply explained that she needed to pray for her ex-husband. She needed to ask God to bless him physically, financially, Spiritually, and in any other way she could think that he would need blessing. We prayed, and she committed to pray each and every day for him. The church also provided some much-needed assistance.

Three days later she came bursting back into my office holding a check for $800 from her ex-husband. She had received the check that day, but it had been mailed on the very day she began to pray. She said, "I am going home right now to start asking God to bless his sex life."

*Dear Lord, I will not dwell on the past. Please forgive me the sin of acting like I am God. I accept the full responsibility for holding on to my anger and unforgiving heart. I ask you to forgive me for not letting you free me from my past pain. I will not hold on to the pain in my past. I give it to you Lord Jesus. I will not replay the pain over and over in my mind. I will not talk to others about the past pain dragging them into my pain. I will share the hope of your restoration. I will not let this pain in my past stand between Your will and my future. I know when you wash me I will be whiter than snow. I will no longer sit in the jail cell of unforgiveness or the table of poverty. When I open my mouth, it will be only to tell of the joy I have found in you, dear Jesus. You alone have the key to my jail cell of pain, not the jailer. I now hand the person of my past pain to you. They are your responsibility not mine. I will start by asking you to bless all those who forced their abnormal sin in my life. I ask that you bless every detail of their life to the point of Spiritual conviction. I also ask that you richly and deeply bless me. I ask you to bless me Spiritually, mentally, and physically. Give me the Spiritual wisdom to rest in your loving arms gentle Jesus.*

*Your Servant's Prayer*

# Chapter 8

## The Seed of Knowledge Always Has a Price

*The 5 Rules of the Harvest:*
1. *You reap what you sow*
2. *You reap exactly what you sow*
3. *You reap each and every time you sow*
4. *You reap more than you sow*
5. *You reap later than you sow*

The Bible is overflowing with seed sowing scripture. One of the understandings in the science of Bible study is that if words or concepts are taught more than once, then you should pay very close attention. In science, a one time event is a Spiritual miracle; for example, the virgin birth of Jesus Christ. If an idea, concept or word occurs over and over again, then, just like science, it is a fact. Scientific facts can be counted, measured, and studied, and experiments can be conducted. The science of Bible study operates under the same rules. When the Word of God repeats a concept, like the five laws of the harvest, the Bible directs us to pay extra special attention to the facts. The question is, "What are the facts?" What reality is God trying to teach you and me?

I challenge you to go to any Bible search program and type in words like harvest, seed, sow, reap, plant, pick, tree, ground, season, harvest time, sower, vine, vine dresser, field, or Lord of the harvest. The Word of God makes it clear. These laws, rules, and absolutes are facts. Before man attempted to understand science, God operated the universe and all creation by these laws. Sir Isaac Newton's laws of motion are three physical laws that form the idea of cause and effect. He formulated these laws based on the natural laws of the harvest, which he first learned from the Bible. To paraphrase Newton, "You must have first cause then effect."

## Scripture Verses: Rules of The Harvest

(Some of the many scriptural references to sowing and reaping)

**1. You reap what you sow:** Galatians 6:7, *"Do not be deceived, God is not mocked; for whatever a man sows, this he will also reap."*

**2. You reap exactly what you sow:** Matthew 13: 31 – 32, *"He told them another parable: The kingdom of heaven is like a mustard seed, which a man took and planted in his field. Though it is the smallest of all your seeds, yet when it grows, it is the largest of garden plants and becomes a tree, so that the birds of the air come and perch in its branches."*

**3. You reap each and every time you sow:** II Corinthians 9:6 – 7, *"But this I say, He that sowed scarcely shall reap also scarcely; and he that sowed abundantly shall reap also abundantly. Let each man do according as he hath purposed in his heart: not grudgingly, or of necessity: for God love's a cheerful giver."*

**4. You reap more than you sow:** II Corinthians 9:6, *"But this I say, He which sowed scarcely shall reap also scarcely; and he which sowed abundantly shall reap also abundantly."*

**5. You reap later than you sow:** James 5:6 – 8, *"Therefore be patient, brethren, until the coming of the Lord. The farmer waits for the precious produce of the soil, being patient about it, until it gets the early and late rains. You too be patient; strengthen your hearts, for the coming of the Lord is near."*

## Apply The Harvest Rules

The reality is that we cannot do anything about last year's harvest. However, we can do something about this year's harvest, and we can start today. Christ Centered Reality stresses that we must stop being a hostage of the past abnormal reality. We live in the here and now. It is easier to redirect the living than to resurrect the dead.

The choices we make today will determine the outcome of the future. Your past abnormal reality has produced your present life events. Normal reality can have a greater impact on the present simply due to the fact that people live life in the present, not in the past. The longer we cling to and dwell in the past problems, the larger the crop of problems we will harvest.

## Results of The Harvest

In the harvest system, God will utilize your gifts and talents to meet your needs and optimize your effectiveness. John 4:35 – 38 tells us that, *"One sows, another reaps."* The sowing is the harder work. God always picks the season for the harvest. God will appoint the optimal time for you to harvest. All seasons are not the same length of time.

John 4:35 – 38, *"Don't you say, 'There are still four more months, then comes the harvest? Listen [to what] I'm telling you: Open your eyes and look at the fields, for they are ready for harvest. The reaper is already receiving pay and gathering fruit for eternal life, so the sower and reaper can rejoice together. For in this case the saying is true: One sows and another reaps. I sent you to reap what you didn't labor for; others have labored, and you have benefited from their labor."*

There have literally been thousands of stories of missionaries who spent their life's work plowing the ground and sowing the seeds, but who saw very little reward for their effort. Then the next missionary who followed in their footsteps would experience a huge explosion of new Christians. The harvest would expand beyond any scope of reason. You do not need to look for the harvest. God will open your eyes and you will see the direction of the harvest. We reap only what has been sown. In Galatians 6:8, Paul is writing to the Galatians, warning them not to mix their seeds. *"...because the one who sows to his flesh will reap corruption from the flesh, but the one who sows to the Spirit will reap eternal life from the Spirit."* In the parable of the wheat and the weeds, Jesus explains the enemy of the harvest. Matthew 13:24 – 26, *"The kingdom of heaven may be compared to a man who sowed good seed in his field. But while people were sleeping, his enemy came, sowed weeds among the wheat, and left. When the plants sprouted and produced grain, then the weeds also appeared."* The enemy is always waiting to confuse, discourage, and sow evil into your good work. The enemy follows God's laws of the harvest because the enemy knows how effectively the laws work.

God follows His rules of the harvest. God is also sovereign over the restoration of the field, season, and crop harvested. Jesus is the boss, not us! In 1874, Knowles Shaw, inspired by Psalm 126:6, expressed the restoring power of "The Lord of The Harvest" in the old Spiritual hymn, "Bringing in the Sheaves,"

*"Sowing in the morning, sowing seeds of kindness, Sowing in the noontide and the dewy eve; Waiting for the harvest, and the time of reaping, We shall come rejoicing, bringing in the sheaves. Bringing in the sheaves, bringing in the sheaves, We shall come rejoicing, bringing in the sheaves, Bringing in the sheaves, bringing in the sheaves, We shall come rejoicing, bringing in the sheaves."*

David also understood the healing power of God. He understood that God can and will restore tragedy into joy, poverty into wealth, and sickness into health. In Psalm 126: 4 – 6 he wrote, *"Restore our fortunes, LORD, like watercourses in the Negev. Those who sow in tears will reap with shouts of joy. Though one goes along weeping, carrying the bag of seed, he will surely come back with shouts of joy, carrying his sheaves."*

Harvesting is hard work. You must keep the weeds out because that is what is best for the plant, and it makes the crop easier to harvest when it is time. My grandfather was a man of the earth who had a large garden. When he was in his 70's, I would join him in the field chopping weeds between the rows of plants. He would be halfway down the row and still not even breathing hard. I would be at the head of the row, huffing and puffing. I did not understand until much later that he kept a file in his back pocket. He used the file about every four or five minutes, and he would say, "Hit that hoe blade and keep it sharp." He not only kept the rows clean; he kept his tools sharp. Martin Luther understood the need to keep his tools sharp; *"I have so much to do today that I should spend the first three hours in prayer."* Paul is expressing the idea to the Galatians that we must wait on God and His plan when he writes in Galatians 6:9, *"So we must not get tired of doing good, for we will reap at the proper time if we don't give up."*

Early in my ministry, I was desperately concerned about all the people in my life who I felt did not know Christ as their personal Savior. I plotted, prayed, and planned over how I would reach them. Much of the time my plans were like that of George and Lennie, "The best laid plans of mice and men."

One evening many years ago, while driving home and listening to Dr. McGee's Bible lesson on 105.7 F.M. KHCB radio in Houston, he shared a simple and profound truth. Dr. McGee explained that we are not the boss, general manager, director, or even the Indian Chief of the harvest, nor will we ever be. There is one and only one Lord of the Harvest and it is not us. Luke10:1 – 3 states, *"The harvest is abundant, but the workers are few. Therefore, pray to the Lord of the harvest to send out workers into His harvest."* The harvest is the Lord's responsibility to supervise. God is responsible for sending the workers. What a relief I felt when I finally understood that I could be part of the harvest without being the one to have the master plan. Our job is to go where we are told, when we are told.

As a Christian, Billy Graham's job description and my job description are the same. Your job and my job are to go and work. The Father did not wake up in shock this morning to discover how few workers there are in the fields. Jesus advises us that if we wish to see a good harvest, then we need to pray to the Lord of the harvest. All the Christians who work the harvest also receive the blessings of the harvest.

# Chapter 9

## The Ground and The Seeds

*Success begins with the type of seed you sow and where you sow the seed.*

In Mark 4:3 – 9, Jesus was teaching his disciples and a very large crowd about the laws of the harvest when He said,

*"'Listen to this! Behold, the sower went out to sow; as he was sowing, some seed fell beside the road, and the birds came and ate it up. Other seed fell on the rocky ground where it did not have much soil; and immediately it sprang up because it had no depth of soil. And after the sun had risen, it was scorched; and because it had no root, it withered away. Other seed fell among the thorns, and the thorns came up and choked it, and it yielded no crop. Other seeds fell into the good soil, and as they grew up and increased, they yielded a crop and produced thirty, sixty, and a hundredfold'. And He was saying, 'He who has ears to hear, let him hear.'"*

The ground you sow on and the seeds you plant will make all the difference

Imagine that with the start of a new year, God calls you into His office and announces that he has a retirement plan for you on earth. His retirement would last until you get to heaven. With a big smile of anticipation, you eagerly agree! You think to yourself that God's retirement package has to be full of amazing stuff. You would love to spend your last days on earth in absolute comfort. Your imagination runs wild thinking of the boat, the cabin, and all the traveling with anything you ever desired on earth.

Then God says, "If you choose to take this retirement plan, the following will be the terms of your retirement! These terms are binding for all eternity, if you choose to accept them." You are now on the edge of your seat.

God explains that you must clearly understand that retirement is not mandatory. You may choose to keep working on earth up to the day you die. Remember that what you do on earth is deposited in heaven, and that's where all the really good stuff is stored. Hard work and real wealth is stored in heaven's eternal bank.

In Matthew 6:19 – 21, Jesus says, *"Do not store up for yourselves treasures on earth, where moth and rust destroy, and where thieves break in and steal. But store up for yourselves treasures in heaven, where neither moth nor rust destroys, and where thieves do not break in or steal; for where your treasure is, there your heart will be also"*

## Retirement Term 1 – Cash:

God tells you that with His retirement plan, whatever dollars you have given to the church, ministry, and God's work over the years, you will receive back 10 times in cash. The cash will be deposited into your bank account, but this is all the cash you will have to live on for the rest of your life. As a bonus, you will receive (in cash) 100 times all the money that you have given sacrificially, out of your poverty. What will be taken into consideration is all the money given by you over and above your tithe: the offerings given with great joy, the offerings made with great cost to you personally, and all money given with immense personal humility. These funds will now bring you great personal wealth. In Mark 12:43 – 44, Jesus said to His disciples, *"Truly I say to you, this poor widow put in more than all the contributors to the treasury; for they all put in out of their surplus, but she, out of her poverty, put in all she owned, all she had to live on."*

## Retirement Term 2 - Days of Your Life on Earth:

God explains to you that the days of your life will be extended. Every minute you have spent in prayer, serving in ministry, studying the word of God, teaching, witnessing, singing praise, or attending church will be added to the end of your life.

Matthew 25:34 – 40 states:

*"Then the King will say to those on His right, 'Come, you who are blessed of My Father, inherit the kingdom prepared for you from the foundation of the world. For I was hungry, and you gave Me something to eat; I was thirsty, and you gave Me something to drink; I was a stranger, and you invited Me in; naked, and you clothed Me; I was sick, and you visited Me; I was in prison, and you came to Me......' The King will answer and say to them, 'Truly I say to you, to the extent that you did it to one of these brothers of Mine, even the least of them, you did it to Me."*

## Retirement Term 3 - Belongings and People You Are Able to Keep:

God further explains that whatever things, or whomever you thanked God for last night, will be who or what you will spend your retirement enjoying! Your retirement is effective immediately; no do-over's!

What if God presented this retirement plan to you today? If you are reading this, it is not too late to change! What can you do today? Jesus said in Matthew 6:20 – 21, *"But store up for yourselves treasures in heaven, where neither moth nor rust destroys, and where thieves do not break in or steal; for where your treasure is, there your heart will be also."*

God closed the conversation by reminding you that you do not have to accept His retirement plan right now! Under the harvest laws and the rules of reaping and sowing, someday you will have a forced mandatory retirement (you will die), and the place being built for your retirement is exclusively based on your activity here on earth. Jesus said in John 14:1 – 3, *"Let not your heart be troubled: ye believe in God, believe also in me. In my Father's house are many mansions: if it were not so, I would have told you. I go to prepare a place for you. And if I go and prepare a place for you, I will come again, and receive you unto myself; that where I am, there ye may be also."*

*The Rule of 52* is based on my book, *Christ Centered Reality Therapy*, which was primarily written as a textbook for counselors, Christian counselors, seminary students and study groups. In chapter 2, "The Spiritual Nature of Man," I summarize Christ Centered Reality Therapy (CCRT) and why it completes Dr. William Glasser's original theory of Reality Therapy. When Reality Therapy is fully integrated with Christian absolutes it can be reformulated into Christ Centered Reality Therapy.

God created the absolutes of the universe, not man. Humanity's best operating parameters occur when we live within the boundaries of God's absolutes. The core belief in the practice of reality is that we are functioning and living in the reality of the mind, body, and Spirit. The best for our life is the will of God. The reality of God's operating design is the best way to have our needs met and our life conflicts resolved. God's absolutes in the healing process guarantees permanency or a cure, not a temporary fix to your problems.

In the New Testament, each and every person that Jesus healed stayed healed! When you are healed by Jesus and follow His absolutes, then you are really healed. If I had stage 4 cancer and my doctor said, "Well, you may die or maybe not, we will have to simply wait and see." I would immediately get a second opinion. I would be well advised to find a doctor who was willing to try to heal my cancer. I do not need to know how I got it; I need to know how to heal it! During Jesus' ministry on earth, no person He healed asked how they became ill or possessed. All they wanted to know was how to be cured! After they were healed, no one ever looked at Jesus and said that it was scientifically impossible. The critics and doubting believers were the ones who questioned Jesus' abilities and motives. He healed none of them.

Normally, medical healing is a very straight forward process. When you come down with the flu, you try to fix it yourself with mixed results. Finally, when you feel like you are on your deathbed, you give in and go to the doctor. The doctor does not give you a lecture for golfing in the rain; he simply prescribes the right medication and tells you to take the whole prescription.

We want a cure not advice. The reality is that you only take the medicine until you feel better. Obviously you know more than the doctor because you did not follow the directions and finish the medicine. Next, the remaining bacteria alive in your system develop a stronger defense against the medicine. The American Medical Association (AMA) states that, "The global increase in resistance to antimicrobial drugs, including the emergence of bacterial strains that are resistant to all available antibacterial agents, has created a public health problem of potentially crisis proportions." The primary reason so many resistant strains exist is because people did not follow the doctor's orders. They simply did not take all their medicine to become completely healed.

There are two reasons for the revolving door of life's problems. One is that you never complete the treatment. The other reason is that you never start the treatment. It is necessary to be healed 100% before you can be successful. Success in life, family, love, relationships, sex, and money follows the same formula. It is not about how you feel. How you feel comes from being sick or healthy. How many of your children's problems would be solved if they had just listened to you and followed your instructions? How many arguments and conflicts with your children would be fixed if they had just paid attention to details and heard you the first time? God must feel the same way we do when our children do not listen. Our stubborn and rebellious nature always leads us into trouble.

John writes to Christians about listening to God in I John 4:6, *"We are from God; he who knows God listens to us; he who is not from God does not listen to us, by this we know the spirit of truth and the spirit of error."* John is clearly writing that if we listen to God we will be doing the will of our Heavenly Father. If we do not listen, we are rebellious and disobedient children. The other reason for not listening to the Father is that we have not gone through the adoption process to become His child!

Paul opens his letter to the Christians at Ephesus with the fact that they are saved and sealed by first listening, then through the action of belief. In Ephesians 1:12 – 13 he writes, *"to the end that we who were the first to hope in Christ would be to the praise of His glory. In Him, you also, after **listening** to the message of truth, the gospel of your salvation, having also **believed**, you were sealed in Jesus with the Holy Spirit of promise."*

Pregnancy can make a woman feel bad and experience a lot of pain, especially during the delivery process. When the new mother holds that healthy baby for the first time, all the pain disappears. This is why being Spiritually successful is so important; no matter how bad you feel, how sick you are, or how old you are, the Spiritual quality of life can grow.

*The Rule of 52* is dependable and holistic because it applies the concept of total success. The key understanding is that all human behavior is purposeful and all behavior originates from the five human needs. God gives and is in control of all human needs. God designed man to have three interwoven needs: physical, mental, and Spiritual. He also designed a system to meet all three needs simultaneously. In Ephesians 3:19 – 21, Paul is writing to the Ephesians about their needs. Paul is expressing that the Father has, and will, meet their needs.

*"And to know the love of Christ, which passes knowledge, that ye might be filled with all the fullness of God. Now unto him that is able to do exceedingly, abundantly above all that we ask or think, accord-*

*ing to the power that works in us, unto Him be glory in the church by Christ Jesus throughout all ages, world without end. Amen."*

God has placed no limit on your needs or His willingness to meet those needs. Our Father will meet every need you have to His satisfaction. The fundamental truth is that, scientifically, all human needs are the same. Each human on earth has the same mental, Spiritual, and physical needs. All men experience the same needs regardless of society, culture, or belief system.

Human needs are genetically encoded in each individual. The genetic code is identical for all human needs. We all share the need for food, oxygen, emotional intimacy, reproduction, and the list goes on.

Human need came before culture and society, therefore need is the first mother of invention and conflict. Man's need for water prompted the invention of irrigational systems and aqueducts. The need for food created the farming systems of the world. Man's need for food and water was also the catalyst for conflicts over water rights and farmland.

Human emotional needs are exactly the same. A mother in Africa loves her child with the same emotion as the mother in Ireland. When an American parent loses track of a small child in the shopping mall, both the child and parent will experience the exact same anxiety, fear, and loss as a small child who is lost in a rainforest. A husband experiences the death of a wife in Russia no differently than the death of a wife Jamaica. The joy of love, pain of hunger, fear of survival, and pleasure of sex are all the same worldwide.

The perceived individual differences are formed in a cultural context. The cultural norms are individually learned and passed on to the next generation. This is called society. If you had grown up as an Aborigine, you would speak their dialect and eat grubs instead of hamburgers. Do not confuse cultural and sociological learning with the basic needs of man. God, the Master designer, genetically endows human needs.

# The Watchmaker

The Watchmaker argument was written by William Paley. Paley, an English clergyman, insisted that, "If a person found a watch in an empty field, its obvious design would lead him to rightly conclude that this watch had a watchmaker. Likewise, the even more complex design of the world compels us to conclude there is a great Designer behind it. Therefore, if the existence of a watch implies a watchmaker, the existence of the world implies an even greater Intelligent Designer (God)."

Our universal needs are like the intricate workings of a found watch. We are the product of a master design, not random chance. God the Father is our Master Designer and He has a master plan. All designers have a master plan for their design. Man can legitimately ask, "What is the Master Designer's plan? What did God intend when He created man?" Man can also have expectations of his designer, and may question how reliable the Master Designer will be in meeting each need of His design.

Logic dictates that man's ultimate reality and best chance for success is to follow the Master Designer's plan. So what's the plan? That is to say, God being real and eternal, He should have design expectations of His creation. His creation (man) should have expectations of His Master Designer.

It is legitimate to expect a real God to be both quantifiable and qualified. The Father's desire is that man not only follow His plan, but also understand His plan. God means for you to completely understand His will. Mother Teresa wrote, "Let us more and more insist on raising funds of love, of kindness, of understanding, and peace. Money will come if we seek first the Kingdom of God, the rest will be given." She was talking about the Master's plan and design for man. Every time I have had the pleasure of working with a young man who wants to go into the ministry, the first thing he wants to do is study biblical Greek. I always ask them, "Have you read the Bible from cover to cover?" First things first, learn what the Father's master design is for your life and success will be guaranteed if you follow the Master designer's plan.

When man's needs are fulfilled, then it should follow that real success should be measurable. If God openly meets all needs, then there are no secret needs. The Master's plan should lead man to a successful, normal reality. It is logical for God the Master Designer to set the design parameters for how man should have his needs met successfully. All man's inventions have design parameters like what speed a car may safely travel. Even the most abstract inventions of man have design rules: sports, games, board games, roads, education, taxes, and even rules for war. We are the living, earthly reflection of our master designer. God's very essence lives in His creation. This also makes man the most elegantly complex of all creations.

## Man is Not a Hothouse Plant

Hothouse plants grow healthy, beautiful, and lavishly large. Once the hothouse plant is placed in an outside environment, it will quickly die. Man was designed to be more like the old, twisted tree living on a cliff by the seashore. The old tree has deep roots and a strong trunk which bends without breaking with each passing storm.

All designers set acceptable tolerance, intended use, and safety parameters for their creations. God created man with a similar internal master design. Equipment which is misused, exceeds safety limitations, or is not maintained fails. It is not the fault of the Master Designer, the failure occurs from the misuse of the intended design. An alcoholic in Russia experiences the same psoriasis of the liver as an American alcoholic. This is simply the misuse of the intended design.

A car is designed to run on gas. If you put water in the gas tank, then the car will not run. God, the master designer, builder, and owner of all creation, has predetermined what our needs are and with what fuel we run best.

God sets the exclusive measurement of normal reality and

success. Questioning what qualifies God to set human parameters of success is a waste of time. We all fall under the natural laws, which include the five rules of the harvest, the five basic human needs, and the five basic conflicts. The steps in The Rule of 52 include the process of sowing the right seeds in the harvest, meeting the five needs, and resolving the five conflicts.

You must understand that it does not take a village. Your personal success may only be obtained individually. No matter how rich your daddy is, his wealth is not your wealth. Your father's wealth will never be your success. His wealth can only be an inheritance; you cannot earn what he has already earned. No one can be hungry for you. No one can be happy for you. No one can overcome sickness for you. It is up to you and you alone to become successful. Real or permanent success begins with Spiritual success.

Helen Keller once wrote "I long to accomplish great and noble tasks, but it is my chief duty to accomplish humble tasks as though they were great and noble. The world is moved along, not only by the mighty shoves of its heroes, but also by the aggregate of the tiny pushes of each honest worker."

*All humans have the same needs.*
*All humans have the same problems meeting their needs.*
*All humans have the same conflicts.*
*All human solutions are the same.*

## The 5 Needs

### 1. Survival - Physical instinct encoded in every human

The list includes, but is not limited to: food, clothing, nourishment, shelter, personal security, safety, health, defense, and reproduction. Survival is the most generic and simplest need to understand. Your culture determines sociological norms, like what type of shelter you live in: a grass hut on the Savanna or a three story brownstone in Chicago. I would still need food, shelter, safety, and to reproduce if I moved to Australia. If the basic need is the same, then the basic problems that spring from the need are the same. Therefore, the answers to the problems created by the basic needs will be the same.

### 2. Love - Positive relationships; connecting, belonging

Love can include groups as well as families or loved ones. It also includes love of work, hobbies, sports, music, pets, and whoever or whatever you can form a positive relationship with. Remember, this is a need of healthy relationships; positive relationships are not self-destructive. You can only have normal, healthy relationships or abnormal, destructive relationships; you cannot have both at the same time. Stupid is the word I use to describe statements like, "I know my husband is an abusive alcoholic, but he really loves his children."

### 3. Power - Self worth

Power includes learning, achievement, winning, and feeling worthwhile. The list also includes the need to create, generate, perform, carry out, produce, compete and reason. This is a real driving force of the human condition. Some NFL football players are paid twenty million a year to play a game. The need for power is so strong in man that we will pay to watch others win for our own self-worth. It's like I tell my kids, "Those actors on TV got paid to act, but you're not getting paid to watch, so go do your homework."

### 4. Freedom - Free will

This need includes: independence, autonomy, one's own space, free expression, and individuality. This need is the very essence of mental challenges, courses of action, inspirations, dreams, and imagination. Ronald Reagan said, "Freedom prospers when religion is vibrant and the law under God is acknowledged."

### 5. Fun – Joy

This need includes pleasure, enjoyment, contentment, emotional security, bliss, gratification, fulfillment, and physical ecstasy. The concept includes, but is not limited to: environment, ease, relaxation, physical expression, realization, illumination, knowledge, comprehension, excitement, resolution, indulgence, belonging, and the grasp of reality.

**All five needs are imperative, but needs 2 through 5 are the basic needs that form the internal relationships. Each and everything in your life starts as a need.**

Jesus had a lot to say about normal reality as it applies to the human condition, which is called need. John 10:1 - 5:

*"I tell you the truth, anyone who sneaks over the wall of a sheepfold, rather than going through the gate, must surely be a thief and a robber! But the one who enters through the gate is the shepherd of the sheep. The gatekeeper opens the gate for him, and the sheep recognize his voice and come to him. He calls his own sheep by name and leads them out. After he has gathered his own flock, he walks ahead of them, and they follow him because they know his voice. They won't follow a stranger; they will run from him because they don't know his voice."*

The people listening to Jesus did not fully understand what He was teaching. Jesus tried to put into plain words a simplistic truth for His disciples. When a person will not listen to Jesus, it is impossible for them to have their individual needs met!

A boy walked into the blacksmith's shop. The boy watched the blacksmith hammer out a horseshoe and toss it into a bucket of water to cool. The blacksmith said to the boy, "Don't touch the horseshoe, it's still hot." When the blacksmith turned his back, the boy went over, picked up the horseshoe, and quickly dropped it with a yelp of pain. The blacksmith turned and asked the boy, "You picked the horseshoe up and burned your hand, didn't you?" The boy replied, "Nope, it just don't take me long to look at a horseshoe."

The reverse is also true. The more a person listens to Jesus, and the more he really hears Jesus, the more that person's core choices will be based on God's will. The more you listen to Jesus, the clearer His voice becomes. The decaying forces of pain of this world will no longer be the main life motivator. The Master Designer will conduct the concert of your life. Charles Spurgeon said, "Damnation comes from men simply not listening to the call of faith."

All people love to win, and everyone loves a winner. Everyone likes to make an 'A' on a test, win the big race, or beat their family in a board game. Winning is a built-in part of the survival need and registers all four other needs.

Your individual opportunity for success lies in each and every conversation you have with Jesus. His direction awaits your choice. The reality is that you come away with a great sense of relief and assurance every time you pray. You will benefit greatly from personal prayer. If you do not come away from prayer with this assurance, then you need to realistically examine your personal relationship with Jesus Christ.

The world loves noise, and much of the world's noise is unmemorable static. Sometimes it seems like sin is followed by loud noises. Yelling, harsh words, arguments, cursing, deviant music, hate speak, abuse, and pornography are all things which make a lot of confusing noise. Try making your own noise list. Sin and destructive noise go together "like peas and carrots," to quote Forrest Gump.

Spiritual success comes to those who turn off the world's sin noise and really listen to Jesus. Sin has a real voice, and it wants your exclusive focus. When you are actively listening to sin and the noise of this wicked world, then there is no way you can hear Jesus. Educational psychology's definition of active listening is listening that focuses completely on what the other person is saying. The active listener then develops a clear understanding of both the content and the intent of the message.

Sin's voice calls and keeps calling you; it will not give up! The voice wants you in its system of failed reality. Sin's voice is like running water; it is composed of many drops, but it all goes down the same drain. Sin knows your needs and always offers a seductive, false alternative. Sin always leads with a loud, emotional voice.

Sin speaks to the ear of the mind, then the body, and finally to the Spirit. Sin knows how to get you to commit to the practice of sin. Unlike modern psychology, sin recognizes that it needs you to be Spiritually committed to really be successful. Getting you to reject the Father's Spiritual rules is the same as rejecting the Father.

You cannot negotiate successfully at the table of sin. Sin's voice will make people go places and do things that God never intended! **Sin's voice makes it possible to feel good while failing.** Sin's opportunities are never God's will. His master plan or design is for your individual success, not for your individual sin.

First, you learn the language of sin. The second step is speaking with the voices of sin. Next, you use the voice to teach others how to sin. You learn to cuss in school and then your younger brother learns from you. You are no longer just a bystander listening to the voice of sin, you have become a slave to sin's instructions.

When sin's language is effortless, then sin has become the voice of your life. Sin's voice now defines you. The more sin that exists within a person's life, the more a person's vision or future action is sin. When you plan to get drunk, you are scheduling sin openly and using all your resources to facilitate the act of sin. You now have an open door policy for all other sin to come in and join the party. You are relying on sin to meet your needs. Sin is now your master, not a servant. You bow at the pagan alter to have your wants met by sin.

Unfortunately, you eventually discover that the only needs met by sin are sin's own needs. The more personal sin becomes, the more a person plans to sin. With more sin there is more mental, physical, and Spiritual poverty.

Decay and sin go hand in hand. The world is decaying faster

and faster, only man has technology implementing the message of decay worldwide. When the internet was new, I was counseling a man who was addicted to pornography. I asked him a standard counselor's question at the time, "Where do you keep your stash of films and magazines?" He said, "I use the internet to feed my addiction." I realized this technology would become a whole new dragon to slay! Over the next few years I visited with little old ladies and children, who were as young as 6 years old, who now watched pornography. People who would never go out and buy a magazine or an X-rated film were now hooked.

## What We Do In the Dark

What we do in the dark is who and what we really are. If it cannot be seen in the light, then stop doing the dark, abnormal things. Normal reality leads to success; abnormal reality leads to failure.

**Learning to speak with sin's voice is as easy as stepping in dog poop in the backyard.** The poop is real, it stinks, it's easy to step in, and it's hard to see. You know there are animals that live there, but the poop was hiding. It is also hard to clean off your shoes. You know the dog is there, but you are still surprised when you step in poop. Others can smell it on you. It's easy to remove when fresh, but let that dog poop dry and it requires elbow grease to remove. You have to use the old scrub brush.

Why do you let the dog poop dry on your good shoes? When you originally stepped in the poop, you merely took the shoes off outside the house. You had the real intention of cleaning the shoes later, but when later came, it was more work than you realized. Now you have a mess. It is just easier to throw the shoes away and buy new ones. The poop parable sounds similar to divorce! Sin is the same in that it can be removed quickly when it starts. When sin is allowed to linger and dry, it becomes more work to break free of the abnormal reality which is the dog poop in your life.

# Chapter 10

## A Want is Different than a Need

*All those who wait on the LORD will find new strength. They will fly high on wings like eagles. They will run and not grow weary. They will walk and not faint. Isaiah 40:31*

Each person has five basic core needs. From these five needs all other human needs and wants are created. There are five basic conflicts that are created by these basic needs. These conflicts are universal to all humans. A want is different than a need. A want is always driven by culture and society. A need is an individual, natural occurring process. A need is all natural; you are born with needs. A want is learned. A want is a man-made idea which is chosen to meet natural needs. Needs and wants are as different as salt and sugar. They may both go in the cake, but they are only blended; they are never the same.

Each and every want you have began as a normal basic need. A man needs to have a physical, sexual relationship with his wife, but he wants to look at pornography to be sexually aroused. He ignores the fact that 99% of all women on the website were sexually abused as little girls and are addicted to drugs. *The need is legitimate, the want is degenerate.*

There are legitimate and good wants. Your individual needs give birth to your wants. I <u>need</u> a vacation and I <u>want</u> to go on a cruise. The reality is I can only afford a trip to Grandma's.

Failure occurs when a want becomes abnormal false belief system for example, "I have to smoke because I have stress." What you should say is, "The reality is I want to smoke when I have stress.

I know smoking is not a natural need. I was not born addicted to nicotine, but I chose (want) to meet my natural need with an abnormal, self-medicating system the world created." You must add all the reality and meaning into that statement to be honest. The survival need teaches us that all people need to eat to survive, but you want steak while your budget can only afford a can of soup. The soup will meet your food need, but your want is unfulfilled. This is the beginning of abnormal wants. An individual's idea of failure always begins as an unfulfilled want. All real needs are normal. The abnormal wants are relabeled as needs. Basically, you talk yourself into believing the unnatural want is really a need in your life.

The following statements are examples of abnormal wants. "I need alcohol just to function." "I need eight hours of sleep or I just can't make it!" "If I don't get that promotion, I will just die." "I need a cigarette to make it one more hour of the day." All of these are wants which have been learned. The want belief system has been integrated mentally, physically, and Spiritually into your belief system.

The process of marriage and family is a normalized, natural need. All cultures since the dawn of time have formalized the family unit and recognized it as a natural and normal need. The natural, normal definition of marriage is one man and one woman. The family which God designed to meet the need of individuals has a logical order: one man and one woman, followed by children. The matrimonial family unit will meet all individual, natural, basic needs. The family will have needs, and need always creates conflict. Unmet needs create abnormal wants. Abnormal wants form addiction, decay, and major life problems.

A man needs to feed his family, so he goes to work. The natural need is survival. He now has stress from the drive, work, and choices he has to make! How does he resolve or fix the day to day stress? Choice #1: smoke and drink. Choice #2: get a gym membership and work out after work. The first choice is easy and is abnormally created by the world system. Choice two is natural and has positive results.

Abnormal wants appear to be the solution, but they create the individual problems. Choice #1 turns into cancer and alcoholism. The need to work and the stress from work will never go away! Some people want sex, drugs, and rock-and-roll to fulfill their needs. When you want abnormal things to meet your normal needs, your life immediately begins to decay.

You are not born with tooth decay, and with proper, normal care, your teeth will last a lifetime. Tooth decay occurs when you do not take care of your teeth. When oral bacteria consume sugars, within minutes they start to produce the acids that cause tooth demineralization, which is tooth decay. Therefore, the less sugar you consume, or the fewer number of times you eat sugary foods, or the shorter the duration dietary sugars are allowed to remain in your mouth, the less exposure your teeth will have to the acids produced by oral bacteria. If you live on man-made sugar, you will get cavities. The more abnormal your diet, the more your teeth and body will decay! I have spent 25 years working with drunks and drug addicts, so I recognize decay when I see it. The more abnormal the individual want is, the more personal decay will occur! The final brush strokes you paint are the ones everyone sees on the canvas of your life.

A slang term counselors use is "meth mouth." Methamphetamine users have tooth decay. First they get horrible "dry mouth". Your saliva acts as a buffer against acidic substances in the mouth, neutralizing them and protecting teeth against acidic foods like lemons, acid from the gut, or acidic plaque. The average person creates around one liter of saliva a day. If saliva production is reduced, oral bacteria levels can increase ten times above normal levels. Meth dries out the salivary glands. Without saliva, the acidic substances can eat away at the minerals in tooth enamel, causing holes or weak spots that turn into cavities. Other medications dry the mouth, but meth is especially bad.

Tooth decay occurs because meth addicts are notorious for trying to treat cottonmouth with lots of sugary soda. The bacteria that feed on the sugars in the mouth secrete acid, which leads to more tooth decay. Also, meth users aren't likely to floss, brush, and rinse when they are high. Decay invariably starts at the gum line, and it eventually spreads around the entire tooth, eating swathes of enamel at an accelerated rate in its wake.

Meth users have cracked teeth because the drug makes them feel anxious or nervous, causing them to clench or grind their teeth. Regular meth users develop cracks in their teeth.

Finally, all meth users have gum disease. All teeth and gums need blood to stay healthy. Meth causes the vessels that supply blood to oral tissues to shrink. Reduced blood supply causes tissues to break down. With repeated shrinking, the blood vessels don't recover and tissues die. The outward decay of one's life is very telling.

The world has created a system of sin to meet the wants of man. Families from the time of Adam and Eve have provided the model for the five basic original conflicts. There are five reasons and only five reasons why families fail. The core of all failure can be pinned to these five original conflicts.

Normal and natural needs exists in individuals, and these needs are also experienced by all families. When individual needs are not met, failure occurs. This failure is then transferred directly to the family system as an abnormality. Imagine a child lying on the floor crying, kicking, and screaming because they did not get their way. This is what an abnormal want acts and looks like! All good counselors would tell you to let the child kick and scream. Do not reward bad behavior with your attention. Do not reward abnormal wants by indulging them!

## Arguing With a Rock

My grandmother would tell me that, "I would argue with a rock I was so hardheaded." You cannot negotiate with abnormal wants. That's like being a little bit pregnant or just a little dead. Negotiating with abnormal wants is like the man trying to stop drinking who keeps going into the bar. The abnormal want is just like the rock: it will not listen, it will not get lighter, and you will always have to carry the rock.

Jesus talked about rocks. In Matthew 7:9-11, He said, *"What man among you, if his son asks him for bread, will give him a rock to eat? Or if he asks for a fish, will give him a snake?"* In the next verse Jesus explains that God knows your needs and will meet them just like a loving Father. *"If you then, who are evil, know how to give good gifts to your children, how much more will your Father in heaven give good things to those who ask God?"* God will not give you rocks to eat! God will meet your normal, natural needs but not your abnormal wants. God will not bless your crack deal on the corner, but God will bless the crack addict who repents and needs to recover. *Recovery is a normal need, and dependency is an abnormal want.*

I first heard this prayer at a Promise Keepers event in the 1990's. I have committed it to my heart. The author of the prayer is unknown, although many have claimed the authorship. I am thankful to whoever wrote the prayer because they had the heart of a warrior poet and the voice of the Lamb. My favorite line of the prayer is, *"I will not flinch in the face of sacrifice, hesitate in the presence of adversity, or negotiate at the table of the enemy."*

**The Fellowship of the Unashamed** (author unknown):
"I am part of the Fellowship of the Unashamed. The die has been cast. I have stepped over the line. The decision has been made. I am a disciple of Jesus Christ. I won't look back, let up, slow down, back away, or be still. My past is redeemed, my present makes sense, and my future is secure. I am finished and done with low living, sight walking, small planning, smooth knees, colorless dreams, chintzy giving, and dwarfed goals. I no longer need pre-eminence, prosperity, position, promotions, plaudits, or popularity. I now live by presence, learn by faith, love by patience, lifted by prayer, and labor by power. My pace is set, my gait is fast, my goal is Heaven, my road is narrow, my way is rough,

my companions few, my Guide reliable, my mission clear. I cannot be bought, compromised, deterred, lured away, turned back, diluted, or delayed. I will not flinch in the face of sacrifice, hesitate in the presence of adversity, negotiate at the table of the enemy, ponder at the pool of popularity, or meander in the maze of mediocrity. I am a disciple of Jesus Christ. I must go until Heaven returns, give until I drop, preach until all know, and work until He comes. And when He comes to get His own, He will have no problem recognizing me. My colors will be clear." "*I am not ashamed of the gospel.*" *Romans 1:16*

One of America's most painful historical events was the disaster of the Space Shuttle Challenger, which occurred on January 28, 1986. The Space Shuttle Challenger broke apart 73 seconds into its flight, leading to the deaths of its crew members. Disintegration of the entire vehicle began after an O-ring seal in its right solid rocket booster failed at liftoff. When one part of the system fails, the whole system begins to fail; some system failures just take longer than others to realize.

Imagine misplacing your keys. You are always panicked and angry until you find them. The real problem occurs when you lose them over and over again. You know how to fix your problem, simply put the keys in the same place every time. The problem or the system failure continues when you never take the time to fix the problem. You could have built 50 key boards in the time you have spent over a lifetime of looking for your lost keys. You are doomed to keep misplacing your keys and being late until you schedule time to manage the problem.

Even the most organized person will misplace their keys from time to time, which is called an accident. Losing your keys every other day, however, is called planned failure. I have a place for all of my keys, and everybody in my home knows about my key place. The rule is if you use my car, then you have to put the keys back or no more using daddy's car. One time I had to leave for an appointment, and I quickly discovered that my keys were missing. I did everything you do when you lose your keys, which means I "tore the house apart." Finally, I sat down in exasperation at my desk. There, hanging out of the USB port, were my keys attached to my USB drive.

Today my flash drive lives on a separate key chain. Problem solved. I knew I was not going to stop using my flash drive, and I also knew how to fix the problem. The important part was that I scheduled a problem solving time. If you schedule time for everything else, why not schedule time for tackling problems? It is normal to fix problems; it is abnormal to plan to fail.

## The Cornerstone of the Five Reality Centers of Conflict

There are five origins of conflicts, just as there are five needs and five rules of the harvest. You can handle one flat tire, but four flat tires and a flat spare mean help is desperately needed. The five conflict categories exist in a specific order. I will use the family unit to clearly and simply illustrate the five conflict categories.

By the time individuals or families are willing to attend counseling at least three of these five categories have reached a critical stage. Families and individuals will try to fix their problems to the best of their ability. Unfortunately, it is often their individually learned abnormality that is causing the problems. Families would rather eat dirt before considering any form of counseling, and they usually wait until failure is looming. This is crazy! People doing crazy things will drive others crazy. William Glasser, the author of Reality Therapy said, "If you want to change attitudes, start with a change in behavior." For most people, seeking professional help with a problem is a real change in behavior.

Genesis 2:18 states, *"Then the LORD God said, "It is not good for the man to be alone; I will make him a helper suitable for him."*

Buddy, it is a good thing God did. God foresaw all of man's weaknesses and built him a helper. The following are some of the reasons man can't make it alone. God worried that Adam would become lost in the Garden of Eden and refuse to ask for directions. God knew that Adam would never make a doctor's appointment. God knew that when Adam's fig leaf wore out, he would never buy a new one for himself. God wanted man to be fruitful and multiply, but God knew Adam would never be able to handle labor pains and childbirth. As "keeper of the garden," Adam would need help in finding his tools. Adam needed someone to blame for the Apple Incident, and for anything else that was really his fault. These are just a few of the reasons why Adam needed Eve.

I have a CPA who does my taxes, a barber who cuts my hair, and a dentist that takes care of my teeth. You would probably call me crazy if I bought a home do-it-yourself dental drill kit and worked on my own teeth. The same logic applies to the man who goes to the bar, gets drunk, and counsels with the bartender and drinking buddies.

When it comes to the family, which most people consider the most important part of their life relationship, why is counseling not considered? Have you ever noticed how much interpersonal relationship counseling Jesus did in His ministry, not to mention how many outdoor workshops he hosted?

When individuals fail to have their needs met, they will seek out a system to meet the needs. A person with a chemical imbalance that leads to long term depression will seek relief from alcohol or drugs. If the depression is left untreated, it leads to an abnormal system of self medication. Fifty percent of all alcoholics in the USA are chronically and pervasively depressed.

The longer the conflicts exist, the more a person will seek out a failed abnormal system of unrealistic wants to meet their needs. A wife uses sex to punish her husband for not making enough money to meet her wants. Next, the man turns to pornography, then finally to a prostitute. The conflict will continue to grow until the problem is identified and then redirected. First, abnormal wants tear down your normal needs. Then abnormality turns your normal needs into abnormal wants. Next, abnormality artificially meets your wants, which is the world system of sin. The sin system forms conflict, and unresolved conflict affects the mind, body, and Spirit simultaneously.

## Sit down In the Counselor's Chair

Pretend that you are counseling a married couple. You start by making a statement naming the five original areas of conflict. The statement would go something like this, "Mr. and Mrs. Smith, in your marriage are you experiencing conflict in any of the following areas: issues that surround **children,** issues that surround **money,** issues with **significant others, sexual issues, and religious or Spiritual issues.**" What you will discover is that these five areas of conflict are almost always all in desperate need of repair. The five areas are just like the four flat tires and a flat spare.

The following is a detailed explanation of the five original areas of conflict, in the order of conflict priority. Conflict priority is what married couples and individuals argued about from most to least.

## The Five Conflicts:

1. **Children** - any and all issues that surround children, grandchildren, and step children, including: when children should date, their clothes, music, grades, driving, cell phones, custody, birthdays, and Christmas.

2. **Money** - any and all issues that surround money, including: new jobs, job searching, loss of employment, work, too much or too little work, time consumption, retirement, debt, taxes, record keeping, who controls the money, bills, and Christmas.

3. **Extended family** – any and all issues that surround family, including: marriage, friends, in-laws, outlaws, significant others who impact your relationships, divorce, your children, my children, foster children, drinking buddies, fishing buddies, facebook buddies and Christmas.

4. **Sex** - any and all issues that surround sex, including: too much or too little, perception of inadequacy, reception, impotency, contraception, age, emotional inadequacy, trust, puberty, illness, death, remarriage, pregnancy, contraception, privacy, and Christmas.

5. **Religion** – any and all issues that surround religion, including: weddings, births, deaths, baptisms, communion, too much or too little, denominations, prayer, class, tradition, cults, and any or all Spiritual involvement and Christmas.

Before you disagree with these five categories, consider and explore the possibility that these are the only five things people authentically argue about universally. All of the other arguments are easily traced back to one or more of the original five conflicts. Conflicts leave a trail of decay and debris.

All five categories operate independently, and they all interact and support the other conflicts. It's like the man who forgot to take out the trash; next thing he knows, his wife is yelling at him. Then she's listing his lack of money, the lack of time spent with her, and the stupid thing he did at their wedding ten years ago. She ends with, "You just don't love me." What does this have to do with not taking out the trash? Nothing! She is simply expressing that her needs are not being met.

People have the same conflicts over the same things worldwide. Right now, there is some guy in India being yelled at about yak poop on the driveway. These conflicts are formed from naturally unfulfilled needs. The harder it is to meet an individual's *needs*, the more distressed the *want* and the greater the *conflict*.

## All Conflicts Have a Starting Place

The five conflicts allow for problem identification in concrete terms. *The Rule of 52* is a real and tangible cure. Vague humanistic psychology speaks in psychobabble terms. These are colorful terms that have very little practical application and meaning. The humanistic counselors ask questions like, "Tell me, how does this make you feel?" The question is not relevant to the cure! How you feel is dealing with your emotions, not the core conflict problem. Feelings are a byproduct of a conflict, not the conflict itself. In couples counseling, love is not the problem; it is the conflicts that are choking the love out of the relationship. You can love someone and still not be able to live with that person. Bad behavior and love are very different things!

All humans have five needs and five conflicts. Understanding what is wrong is also called diagnosis. A real diagnosis gives you a real chance to fix a problem. When I take my car to the auto mechanic, he does not ask me how I feel about my car being busted! He knows how I feel. I am mad, inconvenienced, and hoping it does not cost too much to fix. The mechanic must first diagnose the car's problem, and then he fixes the car. Once my car is fixed (my need is met), I can travel to meet the transportation needs of my family.

Identifying the five real conflicts is a starting point to repair all relationships. Once the conflicts are identified, then you can develop a clear plan for success. If you have too much month at the end of the money, then you need to spend less or make more money, or do both. To continue in the same direction of failure will create almost unbearable family consequences. A lack of money at the end of each month can result in the car being repossessed, the lights being cut off, or the kids going hungry, which will in turn spark a variety of additional family conflicts. The core conflict is still the lack of funds! You can plan for success or plan for failure, but you cannot do both. I know the philosophical question, "But what if you plan to succeed and still fail?" The answer is that you are still planning success, not failure. If you plan to fail, you will succeed at failure 100% of the time!

A clear identification of what abnormal wants are driving the conflicts is critical to success. There is a clear wrong direction and a clear right direction. Identifying the real needs is essential for making normal, need-meeting decisions. You have to know the wrong direction to correct and change your course. It is imperative to have the right direction mapped out.

The more mankind discovers in science, the more God's absolutes are affirmed. Sir Isaac Newton was blessed with the privilege of explaining some of God's natural laws and absolutes. Today we call Newton's laws physics. Newton's laws are simply explanations of God's order and rule. Consider Newton's motion laws. One states, "An object continues in its state of rest or uniform motion in a straight line except in so far as it may be compelled to change that state by action of some outside force." In user-friendly terms, a natural state of motion is at a constant velocity. If the constant velocity is doing nothing or equal to zero, we say the body is at rest. The earth's forces are constantly in motion, so the only place to truly experience a constant state of velocity is in outer space where absolute zero gravity is experienced.

We can apply this law to the five real conflicts. First, each human remains in a state of rest until a force (need) is applied. Secondly, once a human is set in motion, he will stay in motion until he encounters friction (unmet normal needs). Thirdly, the human will stay on course until individual change occurs. The change is the need turning into *abnormal wants,* then *conflict.* Conflict does not occur before the unmet need.

## Understanding the Cure for Abnormal Reality

Once abnormal is set in motion and left unchanged, it will not self-cure. Abnormal reality will grow and manifest into a variety of symptoms, which can also be problems. Abnormal reality wants and unmet needs are clearly identifiable. Abnormal reality takes on mass and form; you act out your abnormality physically, mentally, and Spiritually.

God is powerful and capable of producing change. An ocean liner's rudder changes direction, but the ship will travel 1 or 2 miles before it actually changes course. The amount of force, weight, and mass of the object must be proportional to effect change in direction. It takes more force to throw a cannonball than a baseball. If you have a cannonball sized problem, you need a cannonball sized solution. James did not know anything about physics, but he understood the power of nature. James also understood that it takes time to change direction.

James 3:4 states, *"Look at the ships also, though they are so great and are driven by strong winds, they are still directed by a very small rudder wherever the inclination of the pilot desires."*

## The Family is in The Boat

In order to be successful, it is critical to understand that it is not necessary to get everyone to go in the right direction. It is like dieting: yes, it's easier if everyone in the family will participate, but you are the one who decided to lose weight. You're the one motivated, and you cannot use others as an excuse to fail or succeed. It is just easier to make the trip with everyone onboard.

*The Rule of 52* is serous corrective surgery. A friend of mine just had eye surgery to replace a lens. After the surgery, I asked, "What difference did the surgery make?" He replied, "I can see!"

The Rule of 52

## Understanding a Subset of Conflict

Dr. J. Vernon McGee said, "Incompatibility means he doesn't have enough income and she's not very pat-able."

The five conflicts can be found in Dr. McGee's quote. The man needs a job, which falls under *money*. The expanding details of the conflict are unpaid bills, car repair, children's braces, school lunches, birthday parties, and coveting a relative's financial success. These conflicts fall under *children, money,* and *extended family*.

The second part of the quote, "she's not very pat-able," falls under sex. The woman has asked her hair salon friends to pray for her husband because he is a poor provider. The hair salon customers are friends from church, and they share with others at the church. She is married to a real loser and they need to take up a collection for the family. The conflict has now escalated to *religion, extended family, children,* and *money*. All five conflicts continue to grow.

## Examples of The Five Conflicts in Motion:

The conflicts of young couples pursuing marriage include children, money, friends, family, religion, and sex. Some of the conflicts are: when to have children and how many, existing debt, cost of the wedding, employment, newly formed friends, families, the guest list, family traditions, past relationships, religion in the church, family belief systems, sex, pregnancy, and trust.

Now imagine an older couple getting remarried for the second time. They also are facing the five areas of conflict prior to marriage, maybe even more than the young couple. Some of their conflicts are: stepchildren, two houses, possessions, existing holiday traditions, existing debt, reorganizing family, friends, and sexual issues. The list is almost endless. It does not matter if you are a young couple from Ireland or Japan; you deal with the same five conflicts because everyone has the same five basic needs.

**The Key To All Conflicts Is:**
*The same solutions apply worldwide.*

**The Five Needs:**
1. Survival- physical instinct

*The remaining four basic needs are psychological:*

2. Love- Positive relationships
3. Power - Self worth
4. Freedom- Free will
5. Fun - Joy

**The Five Conflicts:**
1. Children
2. Money
3. Extended family
4. Sex
5. Religion

**The Five Rules of the Harvest:**
1. You reap what you sow
2. You reap more than you sow
3. You reap exactly what you sow
4. You reap each and every time you sow
5. You reap later than you sow

**Individuals know the needs. They know the conflicts.
The Rule of 52 is the solution.**

The problem is that abnormal reality must be treated on all three levels: mind, body, and Spirit. The cure is that authentic, normal reality must become the focus. The cure will need to be in direct proportion to the size, scope, duration, network, and scale of the conflict.

Brother Jim Stevens shared this story from the pulpit in 1976. "On a hot summer day in West Texas back in the 1950's, a young man walked door to door selling magazines. He knocked on the old, dusty screen door of a white house with a large, shady porch. A lady came to the door with sweat trickling off her brow and a scarf pulled around her hair. He explained he was working his way through college and asked if she'd be interested in purchasing a subscription to a magazine.

She explained that she was extremely poor and had lots of mouths to feed. In 1950, people did not mind sharing their lot in life. She asked the red-faced young man who'd been walking too long in the sun if he would like a glass of milk and cookies. She explained she been baking all morning and would be pleased if he would sit a spell. He sat in a porch swing, sharing his adventures of magazine sales with the nice lady while he devoured a plate of cookies and a very cold glass of milk.

Many years later, the same lady found herself in a hospital, desperately dependent on their healthcare and the surgery that came just in time to save her life. Her financial lot in life had not improved. When the day came to be discharged, her bill was enormous. There were many pages of itemized costs totaling an amount far greater than any money she had ever earned. She came to the final page that provided the grand total of her debt, and written in large handwriting and signed by her doctor were the words, 'ALL BILLS PAID.' It was signed, 'Paid in full with one ice cold glass of milk and a plate of cookies on hot July day.'"

# Chapter 11

## Keys to The Rule of 52

*It takes more than knowledge to be truly successful. Knowledge and action are not the same.*

George Bernard Shaw wrote, "Beware of false knowledge; it is more dangerous than ignorance." It takes more than knowledge to be successful in life; you must also believe. You have been given a grant with unlimited resources, but in order to receive the resources you have to go back to school and become the world's most noted authority on Aqueduct Body Dynamics (swimming). First you would receive your undergraduate degree, then a Master's degree, and ultimately a PhD in swimming.

As the world's leading authority, you would write books and articles for swimming journals and magazines. You would teach at the local college and be interviewed on the radio and TV talk shows. You would be a guest judge at national swim meets. Right at the pinnacle of your career, the United States Olympic Swimming Team would recruit you to be their coach. You would fly to the Olympic swimming training camp, walk in with your business suit on carrying a projector and laptop, ready to coach. The Olympic swimmers would be waiting in the pool. They would want you to get in the pool and demonstrate how to swim faster to improve their performances. But there would be one large obstacle standing in the way. You do not know how to swim! Knowledge is not action. Knowing what to do and doing it are utterly different things.

# Keys to The Rule of 52

In Galatians 1:19, Paul called Pastor James, *"James, the Lord's brother."* The gospels record James as one of the four half brothers of Christ (Matthew 13:55). According to John 7:5, James was an unbeliever during Christ's ministry on earth. By the time of the Jerusalem council, James had converted. James ultimately became the pastor of the church in Jerusalem (Acts 12:17).

The book of James is more of a pastoral exposition than a letter, and it was obviously prepared as a sermon meant for public reading. I feel that this is a "best of" series. James conveyed profound concepts with well-chosen words. His sentences are short, simple, and direct. The epistle of James has been called a literary masterpiece that is both arresting and passionate. James's sermon combines the sophistication and simplicity of Greek with the uncompromising strength of the Hebrew language. James's nickname was "old elephant knees." His knees were literally worn out from many hours of daily prayer.

James was the only pastor to have a letter in the New Testament. Paul and the other interim preachers, while serving as pastors in various places, in reality are missionaries and evangelists who trained others to be pastors. James was literally the first pastor or co-pastor at the church of Jerusalem in the New Testament.

The thing I find most remarkable is who James's audience and congregation were in the First Church of Jerusalem. The list includes Mary the mother of Christ, all the other Mary's who followed Jesus, the twelve Apostles including Peter, Andrew, James the Greater, James the Lesser But Still Pretty Great, John, Philip, Bartholomew, Matthew, Thomas, Thaddeus, Simon, Matthias, young Timothy, Barnabas, John Mark, many of the three thousand who were baptized at Pentecost, and their families. Included in the congregation would be many of the followers who saw the ascension of Christ. Finally, the Apostle Paul was included when he came to visit the church.

No other pastor in history had such a roll call of fact checkers seated in the pews. James had to be right on the money with each and every spoken word. James was the pastor of the First Church from at least 42 A.D. until his death in 62 A.D. This speaks volumes of confidence in James's ability from the members. The Apostles also set an important precedent by having a non-Apostolic pastor as the leader. Christians ran out of Apostles after the death of John, who was the last Apostle.

If this group of fact checkers felt that they needed to hear what James had to say, then we need to read his words carefully. Remember, it was James's congregation who literally wrote the 66 books we call the Bible.

To really grasp what might have gone through James's mind, place yourself in his shoes in a modern context. Visualize yourself as the pastor of a large urban church with the government threatening your life and the lives of every family. The existing religious establishment is working overtime to utterly destroy the church. The church's congregation is struggling to establish foundational truth. As a pastor, you are also working to merge interracial groups from different cultures. On Sunday, seated in the very front row, focusing on every word of your sermon are John Calvin, Martin Luther, John Wycliffe, Jan Hus, John Knox, Jonathan Edwards, John & Charles Wesley, Charles Haddon Spurgeon, Dwight L. Moody, William Carey, Martin Luther King, Billy Sunday, Dr. John Bisagno, Dr. Chuck Swindoll, Dr. Anthany Evans, Dr. Harold Sala, and Dr. Billy Graham, then add the listening audience of KHCB 105.7 F.M. Christian missionary radio. Would you be intimidated? I would probably throw up at the idea and stay home! When you stand in the presence of giants, you better have the right sling shot, the right ammunition, and pretty good aim. James hit his target over and over again. This is why this great shepherd's words are so vital to the modern church and families.

## The Key to Joy

Pastor James writes in James 1: 2, *"My brethren, count it all joy when you fall into diverse temptations."* Why would we want to count temptations joy? I do not welcome problems in my life, and I sure do not need to have any more temptation in my life! What does James mean? What I have learned all these years as a Christian is that the very moment I start doing anything that builds up the Kingdom, the old Devil is right there to dump as much destruction on the building process as possible.

All I have to do to get Satan to leave me alone is just do nothing in the Kingdom-building process. Why does Satan need to tempt you when you're already on the sidelines sitting on the bench? In fact, temptation might actually activate you. You might fall into sin and then fall on your knees! From the very moment of your birth there is a list waiting for you of what success looks like. In school students are told that success is being on time, being at their desks, listening to the teachers, doing work, taking tests, and making good grades. If you do not follow the rules, you will fail! To succeed, we must understand the rules of any game, sport, school, trial, test, or job. No matter how well you run the football across the goal line, if you keep stepping out of bounds, you will never score. Knowing the rules of what not to do is as important as knowing what to do. You will know that you are going in the direction of success if Satan is taking the time to tempt you. When you are tempted, "Count it all joy."

## The Key to Failure

The Rule of 52: Satan tempts us so that we can fail. God tests us so we can succeed! Temptation is knowledge alone. God's test is knowledge plus faith in action. James 1:3-4 says, *"knowing that the testing of your faith produces endurance But endurance must do its complete work, so that you may be mature and complete, lacking nothing."*

James is saying that it is a fact that your faith will be tested! Jesus said to Peter, *"I have prayed for you, that your faith may not fail."* Faith is what you believe, not what you feel or think. Faith is a verb, not a noun. Faith is always given feet by your actions. Your actions always demonstrate what you believe, and what you believe comes from what you know. Matthew 9:21-23 states, *"She said to herself, 'If I only touch his cloak, I will be healed.' Jesus turned and saw her. 'Take heart, daughter,' he said, 'your faith has healed you.' And the woman was healed from that moment."*

Faith is not a reward for good or bad behavior. It is easy for us to think, "If I am really, really good maybe God will give me what I want." We do not need faith in faith, but faith in God through His son Jesus Christ. Faith is an absolute requirement to receive answered prayers. Prayer is not true prayer without faith. Jesus said, "all I require is that you have faith the size of a mustard seed to move the largest mountain in your life." God could have required elephant-sized faith, or moon-sized faith, but instead He picked the smallest seed to illustrate that it is not our faith, but His love for us that is great.

Your child could buy you the most expensive thing in the department store and that would be wonderful. But the real treasure you will keep until you draw your last breath is that treasure box full of baby pictures and handmade cards colored and glued together with love. The faith that God treasures most is the size of a mustard seed. Did you become a Christian to fail? Being a Christian is all about being a success in spite of adversity. Christians can walk in victory regardless of the harsh conditions of this world.

As parents when your child was born did you want that child to fail or succeed in life? We all want our children to be superior to us in everyway. We plan for their success from the time they are born. God who is a rich and benevolent Father will give even more to His children.

Yes, I am a Christian but I spend all my time as a Christian feeling guilty! I feel so disconnected with God. I have heard countless

Christians say things like, "If I just had more faith," "I know I need to pray more," "I know I need to go to church and study my Bible more," and "I know I need to give more." The list continues to grow. People feel the need to generate more faith in order to turn up the power of God. Each and every decision you make is Spiritual, not just the ones you think are Spiritual. Either Jesus is in you, with you, and through you, or He's not! Every decision you make as a Christian should be based on God's will. This is not an act of faith, but obedience. The rules of any game are vital to your success. Do not confuse what you think is a decision of your faith when God has made His rules for success clear.

Faith also produces endurance. Americans treasure things that last a long time. We point to marriages that withstand the test of time as successful. Cars that reach over two hundred thousand miles are something to brag about. In the marketplace we demand to have a return policy if a product does not last. James writes, *"The testing of your faith produces endurance."* One of the byproducts of testing is a faith which will last a lifetime. Faith is a free gift from God, and it is not produced by what you think about faith or feel about your faith. You do not need faith in faith. A Christian's faith should become an enduring part of your life. Your trust in God should grow larger not your trust in the largeness of your faith.

What you believe in is what you will buy, think, and do. Take a belief system reality check. Simply estimate in terms of dollars and cents how you spend money. You will quickly discover that your dollars and your beliefs go to the same place. Each and every thing you do is Spiritual, not just the ones you think are Spiritual. If you are limiting Jesus in your mind to religious things or to the traditions of a church, then you need to rethink who God is in your life. Limiting Jesus Christ to what the world thinks would be like having a beautiful home and only living in the hall closet. Jesus Christ, the Son of the Living God, is limitless.

# The Starting Place

The starting place for The Rule of 52 is mentioned in James 1:5, *"Now if any of you lacks wisdom, he should ask God, who gives to all generously and without criticizing, and it will be given to him."*
Wisdom is Spiritual knowledge. Spiritual wisdom moves the benchmark beyond common knowledge. Spiritual wisdom is experienced by you and others. Spiritual wisdom always leads to action, and it expresses itself through deep, profound belief. If I gave you a list and the list contained the instructions for your personal success, would you want the list? The directions on the list simply said follow each and every step, and then repeat until you achieve success. All things are Spiritual and from God. Nothing God created is exempt from His Spiritual rule. Therefore the instructions apply to each and every thing and person in your life.

The enlargement of faith deposits knowledge that is unobtainable, except through Spiritual wisdom. God is giving each Christian a blank check and telling us to write in the amount of Spiritual wisdom we desire. Solomon filled out his check when he asked for wisdom, and he became successful beyond his wildest dreams. King David was given a blank check of Spiritual wisdom, and he became the man after God's own heart. To me, they were successful as long as they sought after Spiritual wisdom. When they stopped seeking God and used their own knowledge and power, they failed. God will give you Spiritual wisdom to be successful. God will give you Spiritual wisdom to get out of failure. God will never give you Spiritual wisdom to sin. You and I already have enough of that knowledge.

I cannot have faith or Spiritual wisdom for you. I may write, teach, preach, share, read, and repeat Spiritual wisdom or faith, but I cannot give them; no more than a military man who receives the Congressional Medal of Honor may give his deeds of heroism away. He may give you his medal, but you did not earn it.

We pay for what we really believe. Often we spend what we can barely afford to spend. The following story is a tribute to our valiant troops and what they believe. The events were reported by Army Reserve Chaplain Jim Higgins, who is also the Senior Pastor of McEachern Memorial United Methodist Church in Powder Springs, Georgia. In May of 2007, he was stationed at Camp Anaconda, which is a large U.S. base near Balad. It is one of the largest airbases in Iraq. The Chaplin shared that the National Anthem is played before every film in the military theater, and all the soldiers stand at attention during the anthem. The National Anthem was playing before "Spiderman 3." One-thousand soldiers were all standing at attention, but the recording stopped. The men all continued to stand at attention. The music started again, but then stopped once more. Then one of the soldiers started singing, and soon all 1000 men joined in, completing the anthem. We fight for what we really believe. Some fight with money, some with words, and some with their lives.

## The Discipline

The discipline of The Rule of 52 in James 1:6-7, *"But let him ask in faith, nothing wavering. For he that wavers is like a wave of the sea driven with the wind and tossed. For let not that man thinks that he shall receive anything of the Lord."*

The word discipline is thrown around in the 21st century by journalists, politicians, and health clubs as a marketing tool. Discipline is what artists have, what musicians do, what athletes become, and is what the U.S. Military lives by. Discipline is different than punishment. Punishment is what convicted felons receive. Punishment has very low expectations, whereas discipline requires the highest standard of achievement. Study the lifestyles and habits of very successful people throughout history and you will soon discover the very cornerstone of their achievements was discipline and a relentless pursuit of their craft and trade.

## The Man Who Fears Success

The man who fears success of The Rule of 52 is found in James 1:8, *"A double minded man is unstable in all his ways."* Knowledge without action is empty. Faith without belief is unstable. Salvation is not man rejecting sin; salvation is God's grace washing man clean, and then God giving man the power over sin. Paul writes to the Romans in Romans 8:37, *"But in all these things we overwhelmingly conquer through Him who loved us."*

## A Real Mickey Mouse Wristwatch

The wristwatch is not worn by many people today. The timepiece has been replaced by techno-gadgets. In my day, watches were a right of passage. They were given to a child deemed old enough to be responsible and to have mastered the skill of reading the clock hands.

Just for fun, if you have a wristwatch on, please remove it and place it on the opposite wrist. Keep the watch on the opposite wrist throughout the rest of the story. I know how weird and uncomfortable the watch feels. Wearing the watch on the untrained wrist is like writing with the opposite hand.

I remember my first watch. It was presented to me at my seventh birthday party. It was a Mickey Mouse watch that my mother had saved industriously to purchase. I opened my prized package and showed it off to the group of birthday buddies, much to their envy.

I quickly strapped the little red band on my wrist. Of course, being a right-handed, seven-year-old boy, I placed the watch on my right wrist. My mother immediately said, "No! You wear the watch on your left hand." I asked the question that all seven-year-olds would ask, "Why?" My mother, (her voice being next to God) explained with great passion, "Because you are right-handed, you will scratch the watch due to the fact that you do everything with your right hand." This was all the explanation I needed, it was settled.

For the next several wristwatch wearing years, I would wear my watch on my left wrist. Then one magical day I took a course in statistics and began to understand that I had two hands! Statistically speaking, there was a 50-50 chance that the watch would be scratched regardless of which arm I wore it on.

My grandmother on my mother's side was still alive and quite intuitive. I stopped by for a visit because she loved to talk about her childhood and all the things she had experienced during Reconstruction.

She had always worn a lady's wristwatch just as all ladies had in her day. I asked her which wrist she wore her watch on. I already knew the answer as it was firmly attached to her left wrist. She said, "On my left wrist, of course." Being an inquisitive teenager, I asked the natural question, "Why?" My grandmother replied, "My mother told me to wear it on my left wrist because I am right-handed and it would get scratched on my right wrist." The mythology of the wristwatch was passed on from my grandmother to my mother and from my mother to me. I did not get to pass it on to my children because now all kids use their cell phones as watches.

The fact is, I still wear my watch on my left hand, even though I have the exclusive free knowledge that I could wear it on either. It takes a force greater than knowledge to change a learned reality.

Have you ever wondered how many subtle things you learned that you are passing along to your children? Knowledge of right and wrong does not change the wrong or implement the right.

Jesus Christ was faced with the same watered-down definition of sin in His earthly ministry that 21st people are faced with today. Jesus was trying to teach his followers and lead them to an understanding that it is the action of the heart and mind that is the centerpiece of man. All sexual attraction begins first as a thought. God gave man a mind he can control. The mind is in control of all functions in the body including your emotions. Jesus is teaching you and me that the outward physical action expressed by lust is not the cause of the sin. The action of lust is only the end product of our mind.

There is a very fine line between temptation and sin. Temptation is not sin! Temptation becomes sin when you cross the line. A two lane road with a double yellow line means do not pass or cross into the other lane. Temptation is that line once you have crossed you are in danger of a head on collision.

Temptation not acted upon is clearly not sin. Temptation is always the doorway to sin and an abnormal reality. The devil vigorously tried to tempt Jesus while He was on earth, but Jesus resisted the devil's offers. When Jesus said no to the temptation, the devil retreated like a coward.

Jesus Christ repeatedly warned, encouraged, and advised His disciples to pray that they would not enter into temptation. He was saying do not cross the line! He explained that if they avoided temptation, they would not have to go through the test.

Temptation is the opportunity and gateway to sin. Satan plans for our failure. Unless we fight against temptation, Satan will just keep adding to the test until we fail. The way to win is to simply refuse to take the test. That is how Jesus beat Satan every time. Simply turn the old devil down and refuse to take the temptation test.

Pastor James clears up a critical point about temptation. The origin of temptation is not, and can never be from God. The Father cannot sin due to the fact that He is God and is perfect. The Father's goal is to lead you into His perfect kingdom. Why would He want to lead you into temptation so that you can fail? Do not blame God for temptation. The origin of temptation is sin and our own evil desires. The manipulator of desires is Satan. You sin because you want to sin. Pastor James explains it best in James 1:12-14:

*"Blessed is a man who endures trials (temptation), because when he passes the test he will receive the crown of life that He has promised to those who love Him. No one undergoing a trial (temptation) should say, 'I am being tempted by God.' For God is not tempted by evil, and He Himself doesn't tempt anyone, but each person is tempted when he is drawn away and enticed by his own evil desires (sin)."*

## The Reality Keys of the Rule of 52

The reality of a starting place is Spiritual wisdom

The reality of unwavering discipline

The reality that knowledge and action are absolutely not the same

The reality that you must hold success in your arms and love it, and you must never fear success

The reality that with God there will be success, without God there will not be success

The reality that God created man to succeed, and that sin invented man's failure

The reality is that Satan tempts us so that we will fail. God will turn sin's temptation into a Spiritual test. Then God will turn the Spiritual test into success.

In 1 Corinthians 10:12-14, Paul shed light on God's promises about temptation, testing, and what we can expect, *"Therefore, whoever thinks he stands must be careful not to fall! No temptation has overtaken you except what is common to humanity. God is faithful and He will not allow you to be tempted beyond what you are able, but with the temptation He will also provide a way of escape, so that you are able to bear it."*

# Chapter 12

## The Art of the Rubber Chicken

*I received an e-mail that included this parable. An atheist filed a lawsuit objecting to Easter and Passover celebrations. The primary complaint was that atheists had no holiday to celebrate. The judge dismissed the case and stated that atheists do have their own holiday each year: April Fool's Day. Psalm 14:1 tells us, "The fool says in his heart, 'God does not exist.'"*

## The Art of the Rubber Chicken

From the time I was a child, the rubber chicken has been a staple of humor in my family. The real humor of the rubber chicken is its utter uselessness and absurdity. In our home, we have rules about proper use of the rubber chicken. Rule 1: when you are the recipient of said rubber chicken, you must return the chicken in similar condition. Rule 2: you must not throw the chicken into the trash, garbage disposal, and/or the paper shredder. Those are the rules, everything else is fair game.

My children and I each own a rubber chicken. This provides for equal opportunity rubber chicken jokes. The rubber chicken has a springy quality and will pop out when packaged just right. This is part of the ninja skills of the rubber chicken. Rubber chicken skills are learned only with time and experience. The chicken has popped out of backpacks at school in class (that's my favorite), which leads to many questions from the teacher. A coffee cup pulled from the kitchen cabinet, a defrosting turkey at thanksgiving, purses in shopping malls, briefcases, suit pockets from the pulpit, and lunch boxes are all possible hiding places for the chicken. Placement of said chicken must be done with daring, in secret, and with great stealth. I am so thankful to God for creating man fully ready to laugh. Ask any evolutionist to explain how laughter evolved! Then plant a rubber chicken in his locker.

I grew up with some guys and we have remained lifelong friends. To call our idea of humor twisted is being far too kind. The practical jokes we played on each other carried well beyond our teenage years. They oozed their way into our adulthood. As alleged adults, we came up with the first set of practical joke rules. Rule 1: never involve the workplace. This rule came about after one of our friends found a goat in his office one morning. My friend's boss was not pleased, especially when they discovered goats really will eat anything. Rule 2: never involve the wife or children (most importantly the wife). That is also a long story. Rule 3: the joke must be original and not too painful. Rule 4: the "get-even" joke must top the preceding practical joke. The 5th and unbreakable rule: absolutely no one can get mad. That is why the words "get even" were invented. Finally, there can be no real or permanent damage to each other's property. Anyone can be destructive or petty, but our practical jokes are the stuff of legends.

One of my favorite targets was my dear friend McGee. He was a master of warped humor. We attended college together, and I lived in an apartment. It was summertime, and I didn't have a roommate. I came home to a dark apartment late one Sunday night, after being gone all weekend. I flipped on the light switch, and no lights came on. I walked in and reached for the lamp, but there was no lamp. There was no table. In fact, everything in the living room and kitchen was gone. The small apartment was entirely consumed by inky, black darkness. Even the streetlamp outside was dark. Most people would be panic-stricken over such a home invasion, but I smelled the paws of my friend McGee at work. Now with all my "spidey senses" on the alert, I cautiously walked across the apartment.

I made my way to the refrigerator and opened the door. There was light. This gave me the final clue to the culprit. With Sherlock Holmes confidence, I now had a positive I.D. on the architect of the prank. All my food had been consumed, down to the last crumb. I concluded this to be the handy work of my metabolically challenged lineman friend, McGee.

With the light from the refrigerator guiding my steps, I could fumble my way in the dark to my bedroom. As I opened the door, all the furniture from all the other rooms crashed down upon me. My room had been packed as tight as clowns in a tiny clown car.

Normal humans would think that the room stuffing was the joke, but I knew better. This had none of the diabolical overtones of a McGee practical joke, thus the room stuffing could only be the prelude. Finally, with my table lamps plugged in and turned on, I could see. That is when I discovered why everything was moved to my room and packed so tightly. Upon further inspection I could see that every square inch of the walls in the living room and kitchen were repainted the color midnight black.

To celebrate McGee's victory, we took the next most logical action of any college student. We invited everyone over to a black light party at my place, complete with glow in the dark paint. I am sharing this episode to illustrate the depth of our resolve and commitment to practical joking. Today you would call it an extreme sport because of the perverse willingness on our part to plan, finance, and execute these practical jokes with military precision.

Now I am married and living in my own home. One Saturday there was an enthusiastic knock at my front door. Upon opening the door, I was introduced to a sharply dressed man carrying an oversized suitcase. Before I could speak, he announced, "Mr. Barnette, I am here to help start your new career." I invited him in, and for the next two hours I listened to his presentation. He smelled of cheap aftershave, and he shared with carnival excitement about how I could make my fortune by becoming a door-to-door shoe salesman. He provided me with a shoe starter kit and a good luck note from my shoe sponsor. You guessed it: my old buddy McGee.

Do not think I was just on the receiving end of these jokes. The real fact is that I may have been the most deviant of us all. My friend McGee had a nice home in a typical yuppie subdivision in Austin, Texas. It was Christmastime in Texas. Not wanting him to think I had forgotten him at Christmas, I placed a classified ad in the local Austin newspaper. It would run the day after Christmas. The classified ad read, "Private party will pay $ 25.00 in cash for all unwanted used Christmas trees, living or artificial. Must be delivered and placed in front yard to receive cash." The newspaper ad included his home address. McGee had to sit in a lawn chair in his front yard with his shot gun for three days. He still ended up with 50 or so trees, and a faded, plastic Nativity scene. He blamed his neighbor for the old Nativity scene.

Not long after the Christmas episode, McGee called and invited me to Austin for a men's prayer breakfast. He said it was his treat, plane ticket and all. McGee, who still has the first dime he ever made, offering to pay for everything? Boy, did I smell a setup. He really went into detail about the special guest speaker and how important it was for me to attend. Knowing it was a trap, I still went along with the plan. Besides, I figured after my Christmas tree in the yard stunt, he would have to be really creative to get back at me.

When I flew to Austin for the men's prayer breakfast, I half-expected the plane to land behind the Great Wall of China, or worse. McGee picked me up from the airport. I have to admit, I was more than a little jumpy. I was waiting for the other shoe to drop at any moment. We arrived at the hotel and walked into a large banquet hall with 100 or more businessmen. The men were from all walks of life, from plumbers to bankers. All the men were eating breakfast and having a great time in the Lord. The man in charge took care of some business from a hotel podium at the other end of the room. Then he introduced the guest speaker.

With great enthusiasm in his voice, he shared the background of the guest speaker. The speaker was a tiny lady from communist China. If she had turned sideways, you might not have seen her because her frame was so slight. Her name was Lynn, and she had been in prison in China for the past 15 years. She was held in solitary confinement. All that was in her cell was one bucket for waste and one bucket for water. She was fed one meal per day consisting of a bowl of rice and some weeds, and one cup of tea. Lynn was not allowed contact with anyone from the outside world for 15 long years. Her only human communication was with her cruel prison guards. She was held without a trial. Her crime was sharing her Christian testimony with a friend.

Lynn did not weigh more than 98 lbs. She had salt and pepper hair pulled back in a tight knot. Her face was delicate but strong when you could see it; she kept her head bowed almost the entire time she spoke. She could not see over the top of the podium. She stood beside it with the microphone twisted down to reach her mouth. Lynn's English was exceptional, but her voice was soft like snowflakes, which made it extremely hard to hear her words. She was the most humble and unassuming person I have ever seen. She was not afraid, just soft spoken. Lynn was a razor-sharp contrast to her audience, which was composed of large, verbose Texan businessmen. The men had big booming voices, hearty laughter, and well-fed bellies.

Lynn was not in the least concerned about the time of day as she shared her story. She shared about the present day suffering of Christians in communist China. Soon the businessmen began to look at their watches and wiggle in their chairs. The faces of the leadership at the head of the table changed from disappointment to impatience. It was painfully obvious that the advertised hype about the speaker was a bitter disappointment to the men. Lynn was in no way what this gathering of men and their guests had anticipated.

She concluded to a polite and short round of applause. The obviously agitated men were already standing and preparing to make a quick exit. The moderator reminded the men that there was still the closing prayer.

Everybody froze in place, including the hotel staff, out of politeness. It was the group's custom to have their guest speaker close the morning in prayer. Lynn stepped back to the microphone and began to pray. I was startled when I heard her voice. I looked up from bowing my head to see if it was the same woman. Her voice resonated with the power of an angelic opera singer. The small, frail mouse squeaks which came from her lips earlier were now replaced with the authority and the power of the Holy Spirit.

Her words were clear and fresh, yet each word left you parched and longing to hear more. She was not speaking to the men, but to her heavenly Father. Each man was carried by her words to the presence of the Father. Her head was no longer bowed in humility. Her arms were outstretched, wide open to heaven. You could visibly see the light from her face grow brighter. In that moment, the verse in the book of Revelation became very clear, *"The voice was as when a lion roars; and when he had cried out, the seven peals of thunder uttered their voices."*

The experience of the power of the Holy Spirit was not new to me, but I had never experienced it in the presence of so many. The movement of the Holy Spirit is a deeply personal occurrence, not a public spectacle. There is no divine light switch to control the movement of God. The Old Testament describes this type of event as the "Shekinah glory of God." Shekinah means to experience the light of God on a deeply intimate level. The word's original meaning is the pure glory and shining radiance of God resting among His people. It is derived from the Hebrew verb 'sakan' meaning 'to dwell'.

Time moved by unnoticed, and then the real miracle occurred. The very impatient, big Texan businessmen, who previously had their minds on their next appointment, began to drop to their knees. All around the room a deep calm and stillness removed all but the words of prayer. We were unaware of each other in the room. The men were all transfixed on the communication with our dear Savior, including me. We all experienced the mighty rushing power of the Holy Spirit as the dear saint of God prayed. The hotel staff joined in the prayer on their knees. Miss Lynn closed her prayer almost two hours later. There where no dry eyes, and a concert of broken men bowed before the Living God of the universe.

It was then that I understood why Lynn came so highly recommended. Sometime later I learned the details of her life. During the fifteen years she spent in solitary confinement, she was never alone. Lynn had the Father, Son, and Holy Spirit, and they never stopped talking. She would only stop praying for a few hours of sleep each day. For fifteen years, all of her time was exclusively devoted to prayer. She prayed out loud so the guards could hear. The prison guards could not stand to listen to her because when they did, they would be convicted by the Holy Spirit. The real problem arose when the prison guards started becoming Christians. The guards sought out her prayers when they learned that her prayers for healing miracles passed right through the prison bars to the outside world. Lynn said, "My real prayer life kicked in when I learned the power of fasting and prayer." Try fasting when you are on a starvation diet.

This frail prayer giant struck paralysis into the hearts of men and her government. Finally, she was so feared by the communist authorities that they chose to release her. Lynn was freed under one condition: she would have to leave her country and live in exile, never to return. She spent fifteen years not speaking to anyone but the One.

I never played another practical joke on my friends.

*The Queen of England said, "I fear the prayer of John Knox more than the combined armies of Scotland."*

## The Deeper Well – The Rule of 52

*You have heard it said that blind men become very aware by way of compensation.*

Webster's defines compensation as, "payment or an adjustment or wages." Paul writes in Romans 6:23, *"For the wages of sin is death, but the gift of God is eternal life in Christ Jesus our Lord."*

Our compensation for sin is first Spiritual death, then physical death. We are all born physically alive but Spiritually dead. Each of us will stay Spiritually dead unless something changes and we are brought to life. Paul is trying to explain to the Romans that sin has a cost; therefore a price must be paid. We have inherited sin from our first father Adam. Each parent has passed the inheritance of sin down to every generation. Our compensation (or wages) is death, both Spiritual and physical.

Paul further explains that Jesus' death and resurrection paid the full price for our sin. Each of us has the opportunity to be Spiritually resurrected. Even though we are dead in our sin, we can be made Spiritually and physically alive, exactly like Jesus Christ.

Jesus paid the full price for sin through His death. He only had to pay the price once. Jesus alone was resurrected from the dead, and He alone could grant life. Jesus exclusively holds the key to eternal life, and He has only one condition for us to move from Spiritual death to Spiritual life. We must individually accept Him as first Savior, and then Lord of our lives. When we accept Him in this way, we have a new name and title, "Christian." Upon establishing this personal relationship, Christians get a bonus. Being Spiritually reborn, we will also immediately move from an earthly, physical death to an eternal life with King Jesus in His kingdom of heaven.

Under the terms of this legal contract with Jesus called "grace,"

Jesus explains that as His legally adopted children, He will compensate us as long as we are alive on this earth. The only prerequisite is that you believe in Him as your personal Savior and Lord.

Jesus explains the facts of His earthly compensation plan in detail in Matthew 10:18-20,

*"You will even be brought before governors and kings because of Me, to bear witness to them and to the nations. But when they hand you over, don't worry about how or what you should speak. For you will be given what to say at that hour, because you are not speaking, but the Spirit of your Father is speaking through you."*

In this passage Jesus was not talking about how we should act in court. He was not teaching us how to deal with the government. Jesus was not speaking about the people who will live through terror in the end times.

Jesus was illustrating His plan of compensation on earth. He was illustrating the worst case scenarios. Even today, being dragged before a corrupt evil court by your enemies would be a nightmare. Think about the Jews who were dragged before the Nazis, or a Christian taken before a communist court. These kangaroo courts have always existed, ever since the time man began to judge one another.

I believe Jesus chose this illustration so that all generations could understand His message. Painting this grim picture, He states in very plan language, "Do not worry." I can just see the disciples' faces as their eyes grew large at Jesus' words. They must have thought things like, "Jesus, have you lost your mind? We worry about that every day!" Keep in mind that this was a fate the followers of Jesus expected to happen any day.

Jesus said, *"Don't worry about how or what you should speak; for you will be given what to say at that hour."* Jesus was teaching His disciples that He knows our each and every need. He's not just speaking about the needs we know about; instead Jesus is saying that He knows our list of needs in detail. He knows every word we will need and the very moment we will need them.

Consider Stephen, who was the first Christian martyr, and his words recorded from his mockery of a trial in Acts 7:53 - 55,

*"'You received the law under the direction of angels and yet have not kept it.' When they heard these things, they were enraged in their hearts and gnashed their teeth at him. But Stephen, filled by the Holy Spirit, gazed into heaven. He saw God's glory, with Jesus standing at the right hand of God..."*

God did not wake up this morning surprised that we need air to breath or gravity to keep our feet on the planet. Jesus did not say, "Oh no! I forgot to make oxygen today. I better get busy and make some." Each need we have is created by God. If the perfect God created all human needs, then He also created the perfect way to meet each need. God did not create a one-time fix for man's needs. He created a self-perpetuating mechanism called life.

If God knows the detail of our needs, then He also knows the details of our limitations. In God's plan, He will do it for you or He will give you the power, will, knowledge, and ability to do it for yourself.

Man's free will comes into play when we make each life decision. If neither idea of God's plan is present when you are making your decisions, then, "Don't do it!" whatever "it" is you are considering doing.

Our life choices will either lead to success or to failure. We cannot do both at the same time. The philosophical debate about what is normal is over. God's absolutes really exist. There is an acceptable normal under God; normal is what God says is normal.

God's standards are exclusively found in His Word, the Bible. It is not necessary that we agree or disagree with God. The only option we have is to follow His directions or go in the wrong direction. We can't do both!

Examine God's absolutes about marriage and having children. God gave Adam an absolute formula for relationship success: get married first, then have babies. God will give you a mate and solve the problem for you. Then God will give you 9 months to get ready to have a baby. This is God giving you the time, strength, and power to prepare for the baby. Trust me, you will need nine months.

Can you imagine if you only had 3 days from the time of conception to birth? The sheer physical trauma to the body and to the development of the baby would be devastating. The plain lack of preparedness would send parents over the edge. God knew man would need nine month just to build the nest. Even birds build the nest first, and then lay their eggs.

God knows every detail of what we need. He also knows the time we need to grow and prepare. He will provide both. In Luke 12:6-8, Jesus is teaching His disciples how much He values what men need when he says, *"Aren't five sparrows sold for two pennies? Yet not one of them is forgotten in God's sight. Indeed, the hairs of your head are all counted. Don't be afraid; you are worth more than many sparrows!"* Jesus is teaching us that our Father is a God of details. We do not need to sweat the small stuff because He has it all under His control. Aren't you glad that you do not have to remember to keep your heart beating or remember to take each breath?

## Well Technologies

Digging wells was probably the first construction and engineering project accomplished by men. Archeological records place the oldest wells in the Fertile Crescent. Man knew that water was in the ground from natural aquifers which flowed up out of the ground. As populations grew and people moved into the desert areas, men began to dig wells.

Almost all hand-dug wells are the size of two men digging with shovels. To make a well work, all you do is dig down below the top of the water table. Next, you must brick or stone the walls of the well to keep it from collapsing. Man would discover that the deeper he dug the well, the better the water.

The Bible is overflowing with historical references to hand-dug wells. Wells have not changed much in the last 2000 years. Today the only real difference is that men use machines to dig the well and pump the water. One fact remains constant: the deeper the well, the better the water.

My home in the country sat right on the outskirts of town. I asked the man who was digging the well for my new home if the water would be as good as the town's water? He chuckled at my question and said, "Where do you think they get their water? You and the town share the same water table, the earth's water don't recognize no city limits sign. You just don't have all those chemicals to mess up what God has made." I realized that we all share the same source, and the deeper the well, the sweeter the water gets.

The deeper the well, the longer the well will last. When the rain stops and a drought comes to the land, the well won't run dry. When the well is deep, it won't suck sand and dirt from the bottom. The deeper the well, the more success is certain.

Water pump technology changed farm life at the turn of the century. Most farmers did not get rid of the old hand-dug wells; they simply covered the hole at the top. I have received many stern warnings about the danger of old wells while working on and visiting farms over the years. I have been cautioned not to get close to the old wells because of the real danger of falling in.

One of my favorite movies is *White Christmas*, and one of my favorite jingles from the movie is, "I know of a doctor, "Tell about him, do"...... "Sad to say, one day he fell, Right into a great big well,"......"That's too bad," .... "It serves him right," ......"Why speak in such a tone?" ........"He should have attended to the sick, and let the well alone!" There is great truth to that joke. Wells were not made to swim in, for play, to climb down, to dive in, or to live in. From the dawn of well technology, a well has had one singular purpose, to lower a bucket down and draw out water.

Man quickly learned that you do not drink from the very top of the well. The top of the well is full of bugs, snails, cow spit, snakes, spiders, slime, and frogs on their lily pads. The good news is that all the stuff living in the well gives assurance, if the bugs can drink the water, so can man. God created all living things to need water, which is why God made so much of the wet stuff.

Not wanting to chew on the bugs at the top of the well, you let the bucket down a little further. The problem with the water in the middle is that it is lukewarm. The water gets just enough sunlight to make it neither cold nor hot. Shallow well water tastes bad. It is good for many things, but not for drinking. The farmers used the shallow well water to water the cattle, chickens, or the flower beds.

If you wanted a cold clear drink of water, you would have to lower the bucket to the deepest part of the well. It reminds me of the old cowboy song sung by the Sons of the Pioneers that goes, "All day I face the barren waste without a drink of water, cool water. Old Dan and I with throats burned dry and souls that cry for water, cool, clear water." I can hardly sing that song without wanting a drink of cool, clear water.

One of the universal experiences of humans is thirst. All men throughout history have experienced the pain of thirst. A baby's first cries come from the need to quench his thirst and hunger. Once you have experienced the water from the deeper well, that cool, clear water, nothing else will do!

The problem with the deepest part of the well is that it takes more energy and effort to draw your water from it. It is not lazy water. You begin by letting the bucket all the way down, which means you have to let the rope all the way out to reach the bottom of the well. It takes time for the bucket to sink deep into the well. Then it takes more strength and resolve to pull the bucket back up from the deeper well.

Back in Matthew 10, Jesus was trying to paint the worst case scenario with vivid colors when He said, "*You will even be brought before gover-*

*nors and kings because of Me, to bear witness to them and to the nation."*
Jesus was trying to convey that He fully understood their fears.
When you went to a courtroom in the first century, it was not to
pay a traffic ticket. The authorities would take your children, your
home, and your money, and then they would beat you, stone you,
and/or crucify you. And this would be the pretrial hearing! When
Jesus picked this courtroom illustration, it sent real fear and shivers
to the disciples' bones.

Jesus was teaching why we should not worry about our problems
because He will handle them. We must go to the deeper well and
draw from the Living Water before we truly experience this trust
in Jesus. Jesus wants to meet our needs, but He will meet them His
way. Knowledge and action are not the same. Knowing about the
water at the bottom of the well is not the same as drawing it out.

Jesus meets a woman outside of a town. She is a pagan and hates
the Jews. She is also a real hootchie mama who has no morals. Her
own people will not even speak to her, so she is blown away when
this Jewish Rabbi asks her for a drink of water from a well. John
4:7-13 records the interaction:

*"Sir," said the woman, "You don't even have a bucket, and
the well is deep. So where do you get this 'living water'? You
aren't greater than our father Jacob, are you? He gave us
the well and drank from it himself, as did his sons and livestock. Jesus said, "Everyone who drinks from this water will
get thirsty again. But whoever drinks from the water that I
will give him will never get thirsty again—ever! In fact, the
water I will give him will become a well of water springing
up within him for eternal life. Sir, "the woman said to Him,
"Give me this water so I won't get thirsty and come here to
draw water."*

Jesus is trying to put into words that the deeper the well, the
better the water. This world's water can never quench your thirst.
Think about addiction, it always leaves you wanting more. Jesus is

saying that He will become the creative force which will live inside of you. If you just drink from His life-giving water, your thirst for sin and the world will be washed away. Jesus knows bugs and slime still live at the top of your well, but the deeper well is larger and deeper than any problem on the surface.

Jesus has full knowledge of your individual limitations. He knows your inadequacies. He will supply you with enough power of the living water to deal with any situation. Jesus will dazzle you with His limitless ability to operate through you.

There is no limit to the Living Water supply. The supply is constant; you only have to draw from it to drink. Jesus also demonstrated that He has an open access policy to the deeper well. The woman at the well was a pagan enemy of Jesus, and He still offered salvation to her. By doing this, Jesus demonstrated the principle of the universal need for salvation. All people in the world have the same needs. The solution to their needs is the Living Water of Jesus. Anyone at anytime may go to the well, sink deep, and draw out the life giving water of Jesus.

Jesus specifically uses the phrase in Matthew 10, *"When they hand you over."* This means that someone else has taken control of your life. In simple terms, you are out of control. It is a scary thing to lose control of a car on a slippery, wet street. Maybe you have simply given the control of your life to your children or a boss. Illness can also take control of our lives. Divorce, addictions, money, and loss can all become our masters.

The pagan woman who Jesus spoke with at the well had lost control of her life. She had also lost hope and of ever finding joy. Jesus wants you to know that He is interested in your compensation. He is willing and able to compensate the details of your life. Jesus reviewed the details of the life of the woman at the well and pointed out her need. Then He gave her a choice: keep drinking from the same old well or choose a new water source.

When you take a drink, you open your mouth and drink. No one ever taught you to drink; we are born with the need. You do not have to understand the process of drinking or the chemical structure of the water. You inherently know you need water to live. When the woman at the well learned she could have eternal Living Water, she immediately left to tell everyone in town. She had discovered the answer. Have you ever shared with anyone about the Deeper Well that is Jesus? Maybe the person causing the pain in your life is doing so because of thirst. After the woman at the well fearlessly and literally shared Jesus with the town's people, everything changed. The woman changed. I'll bet you my last dollar that the town folk treated her differently.

Over my years as a counselor, I have heard all the objections. "You just don't know my husband." "I am trapped, and there is no way out. The situation is hopeless." "I just don't think I can take it anymore. He will never stop drinking." "I wish I could just die."

The first 3 steps of the 12 Steps of Christian Sobriety apply to all Christians who are out of control and unhappy. "I admit that I am powerless over my addictions and dysfunctional behaviors, and that my life has become unmanageable. I have come to believe that God, a Power greater than myself, can restore me to sanity and stability. I have made a conscious decision to turn my will and my life over to the care of God through Jesus Christ His Son, as revealed in the Bible."

# Chapter 13

## Ditch Technology

*"Whatsoever your hand finds to do, do it with all your might."*
*Ecclesiastes 9:10*

Many years ago, a chronic and pervasive heroin addict was referred to me for counseling. He felt that this was his last-ditch effort to get clean and stay sober. "Getting clean" means drying out from drugs and alcohol and starting a plan of success to stay clean. Sobriety means a person is actively practicing a lifestyle of planned ongoing success and is resolute in their commitment of an alcohol and drug free life. It is like getting in shape to run a race. You have to train hard to run a marathon. Real success is a long distance race, not a sprint.

The man was 40 years old and had been using heroin for 15 years. He was married, had three children, and his current wife was also a junky. He had been in and out of prison. In his earlier years, he had worked as a volunteer counselor for a drug treatment center. While working there, he was using and dealing heroin. Volunteering at the center meant he had a built in clientele for selling drugs.

He did have a job; he was a functioning addict. He also expressed how much he loved his three children. He explained that he demonstrated his love for his children by always waiting until they were in bed before shooting up with his wife. He was currently trying to detoxify by using methadone to escape the insidious grip of heroine. He found no relief from the substitute drug.

He was at the end of his rope mentally, physically, and Spiritually. He had accepted Jesus Christ as savior two years prior to our meeting. The reality of Christ in his life had a profound and lasting impact, but he was still chasing his first high, which junkies call "chasing the dragon." The real truth was that he no longer received pleasure from the drug. He chased the dragon so long that it finally caught him. He knew it was killing him, abusing his wife, polluting his mind, stealing his money, and that it would ultimately destroy his children.

He felt completely disconnected from God and longed to re-connect with the Lord. He said, "I came to you because they said you were tough and that you were a last chance to dance kind of guy." I listened to his history for 3 hours. It was an amazing tale of a 15 year journey of drug addiction. What was even more amazing was the fact that he was still alive. At the end of his story, he asked me if I thought I could help. He was the most committed heroine addict I had ever met. I immediately stopped and prayed, asking for Spiritual wisdom.

With an air of confidence, I announced to him that I would help him, but only if he wanted to be finally and totally cured. He completely agreed with the idea of being cured. I believed him, which was remarkable. When counseling an addict, my counseling rule is that 50% of everything they say is a lie and the other 50% they tell you is just not true. I knew that for him to survive as a heroin ad-dict for 15 years, he would have to be a Jedi Black Belt Grand Master Manipulator. Lying was his first language and native tongue.

I outlined a harsh plan, but the results were absolute at the end. He had been planning for failure for 15 years; now he would need a plan for success. I explained that he must do what I instructed him to do absolutely, and if he deviated just one time, I was finished as his counselor. He could go right back to the hopeless existence and the failed life he had experienced for the last 15 years. I think that statement carried more power than his desire for heroin.

First and foremost, he had to get off all forms of drugs. I would not visit with him further until he had accomplished that single task. This meant he needed to be clean for 48 hours. The list of drugs included methadone, heroin, and even aspirin. In addition, I would require random drug tests at my discretion. I also shared that I would prefer not to have him take a drug test, but rather to take him at his word. As a result, he was never tested once, even though he wanted to be tested just to prove his sobriety. Three days later, he returned 100% clean. His question was, "What's next boss?" I pulled out my list and we began working on his next 15 years of sobriety.

The plan required him to meditate (pray) for one hour each morning. He had to attend one AA meeting in the morning and one in the afternoon or evening; no other groups were available in the area. He also had to attend a church service once per day and twice on Sundays. With 200,000 churches in Houston, there is something going on at some church every day of the week. He had to attend counseling with me three times per week, and he had to attend an AA big book study once per week.

One really hard requirement of the plan was that he had to move out of his home. He was not to contact his wife for 120 days. He could see his children through supervised visits at the church without his wife. He was good to his children, but he could not have any contact with his wife. He needed to work on his own sobriety, not his wife's addiction. He needed to sweep his own porch.

He had to give his paycheck to the church each and every Friday, and the church would pay his bills, buy the children's lunches, provide food for the home, and meet all family requirements. In addition, the church would provide a stipend for him to live on each week. He had to find a new job immediately because his job was infested with drug buddies. In fact, the workers would just get paid in heroin by the boss, who was also a junky.

These requirements may seem really intense and almost unfair. For 15 years he had been ramming a needle in his arm. He had gone in and out of prison and had been through three recovery programs. He had seen hundreds of counselors, priests, and preachers. His life had spiraled out of control so completely that he used heroin to function, not to get high. He was just self-medicating to maintain

2 2 2

the dragon. G.K. Chesterton once wrote that, "Fairy Tales are more than true not because they tell us that dragons exist, but because they tell us that dragons can be beaten."

His abnormal reality was a revolving door problem. He was chasing the dragon of abnormal reality to meet his needs. People who exist in the world of abnormal reality are trapped because they have number 10 problems. If you measure a problem on a scale of 1 to 10, number 10 problems are the worst while number 0 or 1 problems are almost non-existent. The only step beyond number 10 is death. The heroin addict, his wife, and his children were all living out number 10's.

If you treat a number 10 problem with a number 8 cure, you will fail. A number 10 problem requires a number 10 cure. You have to clobber the number 10 problem with a number 10 solution; anything less is just a revolving door. The number 8 cure will help the problem and everything will almost get better, but then the problem will relapse. Relapse is the professional word for failure.

It is essential to understand that the man had spent the last 15 years of every waking moment focusing on using or getting heroin. Prison did not reform him, rehabilitation did not heal him, living on the streets did nothing, and neither did going to church or even the threat of death. He would always get better but then relapse. I call it half-repentance. It's like straddling barbed wire, with one foot in heaven and one foot in hell. To cure his addictive problem, it was essential to spend the next 15 years intentionally focusing every waking moment on the cure. The addiction had saturated every aspect in his life, so the cure had to saturate every aspect of his life. The word which best describes the process is *abide*. Have you ever had a casserole dish with overcooked cheese? The residue can be so fused to the dish that you have to soak it in hot soapy water a long time before scrubbing it clean. This is what the word abide means. He had to change his life direction and soak in normality before he would be cured. Jesus explains what it means to Spiritually abide in John 15:6 when he says, *"If you abide in Me, and My words abide in you, ask whatever you wish, and it will be done for you."*

Ditch Technology

The man's sobriety birthday year is 1994, and he is still clean and sober today. He is still abiding in the 100% cure.

When my son was running track I gave him one piece of advice, "Run faster." This is the key to winning the race, you simply run faster than everyone else running the race. You need to work harder to become faster. This problem-solving cure works with all issues, including those surrounding children, money, family relationships, sexual issues, and Spiritual problems. You have to run one lap at a time; there are no quick fixes.

It is clearly understood that if you could fix your problems, then you would. It is important that the initial steps of the plan for success are small enough to guarantee that you succeed. Do not pull everything out of the closet all at once, overwhelming yourself and giving up. That just makes a bigger mess. Start by pulling a single box out of the closet and cleaning out that one box. The closet was filled one box at a time, so clean it one box at a time.

The plan for success has a simple direction, much like the direction on a shampoo bottle to rinse and repeat. Planning responsible behavior is paramount. The plan is the essential first step to the larger world of normal reality. Successful people finish what they start. People who fail procrastinate first, then they panic, and finally they are overwhelmed and give up.

America's greatest General during WWII, General George S. Patton, knew how to plan success. He shared his thoughts about success eloquently with his army when he said, *"I don't want to get any messages saying, 'We are holding our position.' We're not holding anything! Let the Hun do that. We are advancing constantly, and we're not interested in holding onto anything except the enemy. We're going to hold onto him by the nose and we're going to kick him in the ass; we're going to go through him like crap through a goose."*

The Rule of 52

# If Success Is So Simple

*The question is, "If this process is so darn simple, then why can't I make the course corrections to be successful?"*

Jesus is coming down from a mountain where He has been fasting and praying. He is met by a very angry father who is complaining about Jesus' disciples, saying, "I brought my boy to your (stupid) disciples, but they could not heal my boy." It is obvious that the disciples had been healing others with a great deal of success while waiting for Jesus' return from the mountain. Jesus now looks at His men and harshly reprimands them. The disciples will never forget this lesson. *Jesus replies, "You unbelieving and rebellious generation! How long will I be with you? How long must I put up with you? Bring him (the demonically possessed boy) here to Me.' Then Jesus rebuked the demon, and it came out of him, and from that moment the boy was healed."*

Later on that day, with their heads hanging in a state of bewilderment, the disciples are asking Jesus if they did something wrong. *"Then the disciples approached Jesus privately and said, 'Why couldn't we drive [the demonic forces] out?' 'Because of your little faith,' He told them. 'For I assure you; if you have faith the size of a mustard seed, you will tell this mountain, 'Move from here to there,' and it will move. Nothing will be impossible for you.'"*

Jesus is giving us the real answer to overcoming the BIG problems when he says, *"However, this kind does not come out except by prayer and fasting."* Men simply do not like the answer. The problem is just too BIG; we tell ourselves, "It can't be that simple."

Jesus tells us this is how it is done! Jesus is saying it should be normal and natural for Christians to fast and pray! The reality is that 99% of all Christians have never spent time in fasting and prayer. Don't pat yourself on the back because your religious tradition makes you fast once per year. Do you think anyone really likes doing their income tax or weeding the flower beds? Fasting for love's sake or for duty's sake is completely different. Do you really believe God does not know the difference?

In 2 Corinthians 9:7, Paul is writing to the Corinthian church members about how Jesus knows the very attitude with which you approach Him. *"Each person should do as he has decided in his heart, and not out of guilt, or out of requirement, for God loves a cheerful giver."* Paul is teaching us not to give money out of duty because God does not need our money! Give money out of love because your heart breaks over the same things the Father's heart breaks.

The same idea applies to success. The more passionate you are about a thing, the more successful you will become. Everything else we do out of need. Most people don't run out and hug their trash cans on trash day. How many people do you know who hate their jobs but keep working out of need?

Jesus' lesson about fasting and prayer is not about how to fight demonic forces. He is teaching us that fasting and prayer is so powerful that you can even fight big problems like demons. He is teaching us how to overcome any problem this world has to offer.

Jesus is saying that the supremacy of fasting and prayer is so powerful that the very forces of hell cannot stand them. He is teaching that the deeper well of Spiritual prayer is found in the action of prayer.

First, Jesus is saying that *all problems are Spiritual.* Secondly, He is saying that all problems are not the same size. A fender-bender is not the same size problem as totaling your car. He is also saying that the bigger the problem, the more need to immerse oneself in fasting and prayer.

A football player works out and practices so that at game time, he is ready to play ball. Similarly, Christians need to make a regular habit of fasting and prayer. This should be done so that when the x-ray shows stage 4 cancer, you are practiced and ready for the big game.

You cannot say that it does not work because 99% of the Christians reading this book have never really committed themselves to prayer and fasting. It would be like a football player who skipped practice and never worked out. He only showed up for the games.

The small team really needed the football player in the game, but he was not prepared to play.

Fasting is to prayer what an explosion is to an atomic bomb. Jesus is telling us fasting and prayer is the deeper well. Doing the possible thing requires the prayer designed to defeat the impossible.

When you lead a person to the knowledge of salvation and a new life in Jesus Christ, you are literally resurrecting the dead. When someone is sick and you pray, you are literally involved in the healing process. When a person overcomes the grip of addiction and you offer intercessory prayers for them, you have literally helped cast out and tear down the demonic strongholds in their life.

Jesus tells us why we are not taking back this world from the forces of evil. Jesus has already beaten the demonic forces, they just don't know when to quit. The disciples ask the same question we ask today, "Why?" "*Why couldn't we drive the demon out of the boy?*"

Jesus answered, "*Because of your little faith. For I assure you, if you have faith the size of a mustard seed, you will tell this mountain, 'Move from here to there,' and it will move. Nothing will be impossible for you.*" Jesus is plainly saying that nothing will be impossible. To restate this in positive terms, all things will be possible. So Jesus is either lying or telling the truth. Either all things are possible or they are not! When you have the power to resurrect the dead, you can do pretty much anything!

Jesus said that there are some prerequisites. First, you have to have a personal relationship with Him as savior. Secondly, you have to learn to draw your power and strength from the Spiritually deeper well. That means you are not self-reliant, but instead fully reliant on Jesus. Thirdly, to defeat the really big problems of life you must learn the skill of fasting and prayer. Lastly, you must have a speck of dust-sized faith. Aren't you glad Jesus said that all you need is faith the size of a mustard seed and not cow-sized faith to move mountains! Most of us have enough trouble with the mustard seed.

I was thinking over a problem with my friend Brian, who is also a church elder. He said, "I have my mustard seed in my pocket, and

I am ready to go!" What an attitude of success! The phrase stuck with me. When you see a problem, take out the mustard seed of faith and overcome the impossible.

Draw that mustard seed like a cowboy in a western movie draws his six shooters to hit the problem between the eyes. In the movies, a cowboy's six shooter never runs out of bullets. Similarly, the power of the Holy Spirit is the living well which never runs dry. The really big fires in life take a lot of water to put out. The Living Water from the deeper well is needed to extinguish the Spiritual fire of hell. After the house fire is out, the rebuilding process begins. The living water washes us clean and heals us.

Given the chance to build a new home after a house fire, we will always try to build the house bigger and better. Only a fool would rebuild their new home with the same old defects and problems. Even more incredible are the Christians who have been given a blank check to rebuild their home after a fire, and who decide to just sit and live among the ruins of the burned out home. These ruin dwellers are the saddest of all.

## Ditch technology

*The question is: why do so many people get stuck in a ditch and not seem to be able to climb out to save their life?*

Well Technology came first, but man, being naturally lazy, invented ditch technology. Ditches are always built by man to redirect the flow of water. Do not confuse natural running water with manmade ditches.

Manmade ditches rise and fall with rain and water runoff. All ditches collect trash and debris. Ditches are full of runoff pollution and everything from insecticides to motor oil. No homeowner ever looked at a drainage ditch and said, "How beautiful! Please landscape my yard with a ditch."

In fact, drainage ditches come with a warning. The water in a ditch can move so fast it will suck you under. Ditches are things you can fall into and get stuck. James, a recovering alcoholic and Christian friend, said his goal when he would drive drunk was to, "keep it between the ditches." Even drunks know to avoid the ditches.

The ditch will not completely drain, and the water that is left becomes stagnate. It grows a healthy crop of mosquitoes. The ditch water kills the grass under the water and leaves smelly slime mixed with trash.

Foolish parents let their children play in the filthy, open ditch. Some children are warned to stay out of the ditch because it can be dangerous, and sometimes they rebel and play in it anyway. They play with makeshift paper boats and run up and down the ditch. Then they return home like the little prodigal children; cold, wet, and sick.

For centuries, the idea was that ditch digging was not something to aspire to. This was the back-breaking work reserved for slaves or prisoners. In Luke 16:2 - 4, Jesus tells of a man who had come to the end of his rope, *"He called the manager and asked him, 'What is this I hear about you? Tell me what you have done. You cannot be my manager any longer.' Then the manager thought to himself, 'What will I do? My master is taking my work away from me. I am not strong enough to go out and dig a ditch. I am ashamed to beg.'"* Even the most sinful do not want to live in a ditch!

Why do so many people fall in life's ditches and not climb back out? Why would anyone be satisfied being stuck in a ditch? The reality is that they are not happy stuck in the ditch. Ask a smoker how many times they have tried to quit. Question the overweight person how many diets they have tried and failed. Ditches come in all forms, shapes, and sizes. They all have the same characteristics and will show up at different times and places. Because ditch dwelling people are selfish, they pull others into the ditch with them. Ditches are never prejudiced; they will accept anyone who falls into their muck.

In Matthew 15:15, Jesus said, *"They are blind men who are trying to lead blind men. If a blind man leads a blind man, they will both fall into a ditch."* Falling into the ditch is the easy part, getting out is the hard part. The walls are steep and the slime is slippery. Many just choose to stay in the ditch. The larger the ditch, the more help we need getting out of the ditch.

Sometimes you need a tow truck to pull your car out of the ditch. For example, if yelling at the kids would make them perfect, then all parents would have perfect kids. Ask yourself, "What is the purpose in training children?" Is it for the parent's sake or the children's need? The answer is, "Both." Children need to learn to function in a family system. A family needs the children to function in the system. Children are not born with this knowledge; they only have needs, so they must learn. And you cannot teach them anything if you are stuck in a ditch. The child's need for discipline and knowledge are not met, thus they will turn to abnormal wants to fulfill their needs.

The jet liner is going down and the oxygen masks deploy. Do you put your own mask on first or the child's? The correct answer is you put your own mask on first! If you pass out before you put the child's mask on, you both will die. If you put yours on first, then you can save the child and yourself. You might also save the other dumb parents who tried putting their child's mask on first.

You can't fix your family until you fix yourself. Individuals, families, and children fall into ruts, or a small, manageable ditch. Another term for a rut is redundancy; having the same stupid argument over the same stupid thing over and over again.

Remember, a life rut is always manmade. The rut in your life is abnormal, and over time it will become a ditch. Every person needs help getting out of the manmade ruts of life from time to time. It is easier to get out of a rut than a ditch. The deeper the rut, the harder it is to climb out.

If a man is drowning in quicksand, you do not jump in with him in order to save him! You toss him a life line and tell the drowning man to tie it around his body. Then you will have to keep pulling until the suction of the quicksand begins to let go. As you begin to pull the person out, you will see hope return to their eyes. You need to keep pulling because the closer to the edge they get, the more they will help themselves.

Soon they are out of the quicksand pit, but now they need to be cleaned up. Once out of the quicksand ditch, they have to go through the cleaning process alone. No one can clean you better than you can clean yourself. Sometimes you need a long, hot bath to get all the dirt off.

The lifeline that pulls you out of the ditch is the plan for success coupled with the act of working the plan. It is hard work pulling someone out of quicksand; do not give up (resolution)! They may not move at first, but the longer and harder you pull, the closer they are to salvation (permanency).

Ditches are always made by man and filled with trash. All graves on earth are manmade. God did not dig a hole for our dead bodies; only men dig graves. The only grave that God was ever placed in was manmade, and Jesus got up and walked right out of that hole in the ground. Manmade ditches cannot contain God's power.

The great Baptist preacher, Charles Spurgeon, has an illustration that aligns with ruts and ditches. To paraphrase:

"Suppose a house is attacked by seven thieves. The good man of the house is armed and kills six of the thieves. One thief survives. Then the good man of the house allows the thief to live in his home. The good man indulges the thief and pampers him. The thief steals the goods of the home and takes advantage of the man's children and wife. Yet, the good man allows the thief to still live in his home. Finally, the thieve kills the good man and destroys his family. If by the grace of God you have driven out six of these vices and yet one still lives, you will still lose everything."

The rut became a ditch, and the man indulged and pampered the ditch. When the raging water filled the ditch, it took the man's family, then his life.

Many years ago I was working at a residential mental health

hospital. I was finishing my work on my Master's degree at the time, and I worked on the adolescent unit. Many of the teens were placed there by the court, especially if they were picked up on the streets. Most of the young men were drug addicts and prostitutes. They were easy targets for adults with access to drugs and money. These young men came in with a list of diseases from aids and hepatitis to tuberculosis; some had all three. Gonorrhea of the throat had reached epidemic proportions in the young men.

The adolescent unit was on the second floor of the hospital. One morning I walked out the doors around 6:00 A.M., heading toward the elevators just as two EMTs were walking off with a teenage boy from the streets. I stopped to offer assistance because it was apparent the young man was still under the influence.

It was at that moment that the young man had a violent seizure and fell to the reception area floor. He began to vomit and shake. I held the teen's feet as he had a grand mal seizure, and he began to choke on his own vomit. Without any hesitation, the medic put his mouth on the teen's mouth and sucked out the vomit. He did this over and over again until the young man could breath on his own.

Knowledge and action are not the same thing. The young EMT was a husband and father of two small children, and he was fully aware of the dangers. He knew the probable diseases the street teenager might have, and the personal risk involved with mouth-to-mouth. He also knew that the boy would die in seconds if the vomit reached his lungs. The heroic act I witnessed that morning has haunted me for years. I often wonder if I would have the commitment to follow through with such an act of raw heroism.

When Jesus was crucified, He sucked all the vomit of sin out of our lives. He gave His life so that we could truly live. Then He walked out of a manmade grave, a ditch, to show us that it's possible. All we have to do is follow in His footsteps.

# Chapter 14

## Learned and Earned

*"I have seen the task which God has given the sons of men with which to occupy themselves. He has made everything appropriate in its time. He has also set eternity in their heart, yet so that man will find out the work which God has done from the beginning even to the end."* Ecclesiastes 3:10-11

The bridge between knowledge and action is the Rule of 52. Success is never given or found; it is always learned and earned.

On my last day of high school, in the spring of 1980, I walked back into the school after the last final had been taken. This inaugurated summer's official start for me and the class of 1980. We were now just a part of high school history. The halls of the school were deserted. Paper and trash tumbled down the corridors from the empty lockers; the school was desolate. A building which had been teaming with life just a few hours before was now void of the energy of youth. A feeling of both melancholy and excitement filled me as I casually strolled to my locker for the last time.

I noticed one classroom light was on; it was my English teacher's room. She was one of my favorite teachers in high school. I poked my head in her door to say hi and goodbye. She greeted me with her usual smile and said, "Well, come in Mr. Barnette. Now that your high school career is at an end, what are your plans?"

My reply was the standard, "I'm going to go to college and then find a job so I can make lots of money." She paused, and you could see the wheels of her brain spinning as she reached in her desk and pulled out a penny. She held out the penny and said, "Open your hand." She placed the penny in my hand and said with a smile, "You have now earned your first penny as a high school graduate. Now all you have to do is add to it!" I still have the penny she gave me. I have worked hard to learn how to add to that first penny. Success is never given or found; it is always learned and earned.

I was married, with children, while attending college. I was also working a full-time job and had a part-time youth minister position at our church. On top of that, my wife and I had just bought our first home. It was an old, rundown track home. I planned to remodel the house myself because I had worked as a home builder in construction all my life. This house was a real fixer-upper. I knew it would need a great deal of remodeling, but when you are young, you still think you are Superman. How wrong I was! The only thing I became was super busy!

A socio-gram time theory is the systematic usage of time allotment in an individual's life, or in plain English, a personal timeline of how you use the hours of the day. If you did a socio-gram of my life at that point, my hours of the day did not add up. It would read like the following: 6 hours of sleep, 1 hour for all meals (mostly while studying), 1 hour to take the children to and from daycare/school, 1 hour of drive time, 10 hours of work, 3 hours of church preparation, another 3 hours for youth events, 2 hours to drive to and from college, and 3 hours study time for college, for a grand total of 30 hours per-day.

The whole "24 hours per day" thing was not working for me! The first thing I cut back on was personal time; the next thing to go was sleep. A real point of discouragement and joy stealer was that there was no time to remodel the old track home.

When my wife and I bought our first house, I had such visions for the home, including big plans to redo and repair it inside and out. The builder in me was disgusted and frustrated with the crumbling home, but I simply did not have time to fix the house. Given the choice between family time, ministry, college, or repairing the home, the house always lost.

The outside siding on the home was the most visibly repulsive thing because it was swollen and peeling. The home was from the early 1970's when builders used papier-mâché siding on track homes. The siding was hanging on for dear life.

One fine, spring Saturday morning, during a dead week at college, I woke up and went to the lumber yard. I bought all the necessary supplies for 3 pieces of real wooden siding and trim. My home repair mission began on the front porch. I tore off and replaced one piece of siding with real wood and trim, but I only had time to tear down and replace that one piece. I used my time wisely and studied for college finals. The next week I found time to replace one more piece of siding. I missed the week after that, but I created a debt sheet. I now owed work on two pieces of siding the following week, and I scheduled the construction for Saturday. During week 5 I replaced another piece and added priming and painting to the project. This project also became family time with my son, Jonathan. He was old enough to help and loved building with his daddy. I bought him his first toolbox with real tools. We listened to music while we worked and talked about father-son things. We still love spending time with each other.

I re-sided, trimmed, and painted the outside of my home one piece at a time. My new theme song was the classic Johnny Cash song from 1976, *One Piece at a Time.* Cash's song tells the story of a Cadillac assembly line worker who took one auto part from the plant each week. The worker stole the car parts from many different makes and models from 1949 to 1973. Then he assembled his own Cadillac.

It took me 52 weeks to completely re-side and paint the house. I began to apply my new Rule of 52 to many parts of my life. My wife also suffered from my lack of time. In applying the Rule of 52 to my relationship, I planned to do something nice for her once a week. My rule was simple, it could not be anything which I would normally do like pick up the kids. The nice thing had to be something which only benefited her. One of the nice things I did was fill her car with gas on Sunday nights, which sometimes included a carwash. I knew that this would be a nice start to her work week and one less task on her list. Occasionally, I would rent her one of her favorite movies and watch it with her (this always included popcorn). The movie thing was (and still is) hard because she is strictly a sappy romance gal while I am an action/adventure and sci-fi guy. This is the toughest nice thing I do for her, but her favorite is when I rub her feet with lotion. I do something nice for my wife 52 times per year without being asked. I never told her my once-a-week plan; she just thought I had matured as a husband. I guess I did! The first time she discovered my plan was through proofreading the rough draft of this book!

I made it a point to spend at least 5 minutes per day with each of my children by providing "Daddy alone time." These 5 minutes helped me meet their individual needs. There were many times when those 5 minutes would turn into hours. This "Daddy time" was over and above studying for spelling tests, caring for lost pets, washing the shirt that matched the best friend's, or midnight runs to the store for supplies for the forgotten school project due tomorrow. This was 5 minutes of individual, personal time devoted to just that child's needs. The rest was just play time. Today I still visit with my grown children, but the 5 minutes has turned into lunches, dinners, college visits, and problem solving. The same rule applied: if I missed time with them I would have to make up the time that was missed. I owe my children my time. I do not get to retire from the "Daddy business." Someday, when my kids have their own children, I will spend time with my grandchildren as well.

The Rule of 52 is simple and it works; it has to be simple to work! It is about investment. Do you invest in a retirement fund to pull the money out the next day? No! You plan to let your investment grow and mature for the later years in life. Similarly, God's plan is that "You reap later than you sow."

My oldest daughter, Tommie Alice, was about 3 years old when she discovered money, and it was used to buy things. A dollar bill was considered really big money to a 3 year- old, and she would say with excitement, "Money buys fries." She was referring to Mickey D's french-fries. The McDonald's Corporation spends an enormous amount of their budget on target marketing french-fries to children; this is why they have a clown as a mascot. They get kids hooked early, knowing that they have a customer for life.

The world system is burning up money trying to influence your children, and their primary tools are time and consistency. Your children's brains are going to be filled, but it is your choice of what to fill them with. The Rule of 52 is all about life target marketing. In secular terms, as a parent you are target marketing to your children. Never rely on anyone else to give life-changing knowledge to your children. It's like President Harry Truman said, "The buck stops here." If what you are doing is not working, change what you are doing! The kids will change if you change.

I have attended many workshops and seminars that are a bit overwhelming. Seminars are full of great ideas, concepts, and new systems, but you would have to have a full-time employee just to learn the stuff. You go home and the workbook, CDs, and other materials just sit on a bookshelf collecting dust. We have evolved into a 'point and click' society. Instant knowledge, gratification, and information are now more valuable than quality. Bill Gates took the complicated language that a computer speaks and translated it into user-friendly English. That was the secret to his success. He did not originate the idea; he simply worked the problem until he was successful. The Rule of 52 is a simplistic way to reprogram your life for success while meeting your needs. When you meet needs of others, the next thing that happens is that some of your needs begin to be met.

One of my key ideas is that most people know 90% of their problems (needs) and 90% of their solutions. What escapes them is the 10%, or how to successfully bridge the need and the solution.

The Rule of 52 deals with problems people are not willing, ready, or able to deal with, but that they sincerely want to repair. Your current behavior is an extension of past learned behaviors. You can be a Christian and still have the same old lingering habits and problems. It's like the man who was drowning and was saved by the lifeguard; he still came out of the water with the same habits he had before he was saved.

The learned behavior (bad habit) has only changed shape, size, impact, and magnitude. As a baby, you learned sounds; the sounds formed words; the words formed meaning. Then you used the words to get what you wanted. Later you learned to cuss and tell dirty jokes. You are in full control of what comes out of your mouth and how it impacts your life and others. When you became a Christian, you did not stop using the language you learned, nor did the old habits just disappear. If you are truly a new creation and really born again, shouldn't your words change? The reality is that nothing changes without work. You have the power of the Holy Spirit to guarantee success, but you still have to want to change.

Peter, even after having been with Jesus for three and a half years, still returned to his old habit of fear. If you study the life of Peter, you will find a man who had to work very hard to become successful as a Christian. It was never Peter's salvation in question; the problem was with his commitment. In Matthew 26: 74 - 75 it is written, *"Then Peter began **to curse and to swear**, saying, 'I do not know the man.' And immediately the cock crowed. And Peter remembered the word of Jesus, 'Before the cock crows, you, Peter, shall deny me three times,' and Peter went out and wept bitterly."* Peter did not obtain success instantly or easily. The key was that he worked God's plan for success everyday! We do not know when Peter stopped cursing, but his effectiveness as an Apostle depended upon his behavior changing one detail at a time.

# Applying the Rule of 52 to Your Life

## Step # 1: Application ~
## Always Begins with a Question

People who are overweight know they are overweight. The person knows the problem; they are overweight and out of shape. I speak from experience because ice cream is my weakness. The individual also knows the solution; it takes diet control and exercise to lose even one pound. Every adult in America knows the answer to weight loss. If the answer is so simple, why are there so many overweight people? This is the 10% part of the solution that escapes us. **The bridge between knowledge and action is The Rule of 52.**

## The Rule of 52 Question
## Applied to Weight Loss:

Could you lose just one pound per month? This is a very reasonable goal, and for most people the answer is, "Yes." Then you would lose 12 pounds per year. What if you then lost 12 more pounds over the next year? In those 2 years you would have lost 24 pounds. Then you lose 12 more pounds in the third year for a total of 36 pounds. How would this weight loss affect your life? What would you physically look like in three years if you lost 36 pounds? Can you start today by losing your one pound this month?

I challenge any students going to college to take a copy of their birth certificate, tape it to their bathroom mirror, and look at it each morning. Then make the following statement, "I can get older with education, or I can get older without education; either way I am going to get older."

Apply the same logic to weight loss. I can lose one pound this month or I can stay one pound heavier; time will march on! The problem with most solutions is that we are unrealistic with our expectations. Normal reality has to play the largest role in success. The difference in planned success and planned failure is normal reality. If you stood motionless in a room only breathing, the one thing that will change is time, regardless of what you do or don't do!

## The Rule of 52 Question Applied to Money:

Can you save $5 in cash per week in your sock drawer for 52 weeks? At the end of 52 weeks, you would have $260 in cash. Make this weekly $5 contribution to the sock drawer for 20 years and you would have $5,200. What if you had that amount of cash right now? Would you ever really miss the $5 per week? What are you currently wasting $5 on each week?

Imagine if you saved $100 per week. At the end of 20 years, you would have $104,000. If you had that much cash in your dresser drawer right now, would it make a difference in your life? The fact is that you can grow older without saving money, or you can grow older with cash money in the sock drawer; you will grow older! You can start today! If you can't save $5, then save $1, but get started immediately. Remember the rules of the harvest: You reap what you sow; you reap more than you sow; you reap exactly what you sow; you reap each and every time you sow; you reap later than you sow.

The Rule of 52 can be applied to savings because money is one of our needs. The Rule of 52 is about total life success and sowing the seeds of success into your own life first, and then into others. You must be successful to lead others to success. You have to do both to truly be successful. Paul writes one of the conditions of the harvest rules in 2 Corinthians 9:6, *"Remember this: the person who sows sparingly will also reap sparingly, and the person who sows generously will also reap generously."* You cannot out-give God, and you cannot change the rules of the harvest.

Abnormal reality can also practice The Rule of 52 effectively and efficiently. Imagine a teenager who starts drinking with his buddies during his senior year in high school. He gets drunk 2 or 3 times per week. Then he goes to college, but he limits drinking and getting drunk to one night per week. After graduation, he is off to the big office job and his once or twice a week martini meeting with the boss. At home over the weekends, he has 1 or 2 cases of beer during a little backyard BBQ, and watches the game with his buddies.

Let's do a Rule of 52 math problem by adding up his days drinking in college. By compressing the drinking timeline into days, we know he got drunk once per week for 52 weeks. He stayed drunk for 2 months per year during his 4 years of college. He devoted 8 total months of his life during college to drinking.

As a graduate in the working world, the compressed timeline would be 3 days drunk per week. At 52 weeks, that would be 156 days per year or 5.2 months per year drunk. If you do not like the math, consider how credit cards calculate interest. The interest starts accruing from the very moment you purchase anything, and it continues until you pay your debt in full. A $2.99 breakfast at 18% for 12 months will cost you $49. Just because you charge $2.99 at a time, you still pay the full price. Proverbs 22:7 states, *"The rich rule over the poor, and the borrower is servant to the lender."*

**The door swings both ways.** The world system uses our weaknesses to trap us into being fat, out of shape, drunken, workaholics, overachievers, money seekers, or self-serving junkies. The idea that I have shared many times with junkies is, "If you can be committed to being a failure, then put the same commitment and time into being a success."

James, an alcoholic, shared the story of his first A.A. meeting with me. James asked a fellow AA member, "How many meetings do I have to attend?" The other alcoholic replied, "How many days a week did you drink?" James responded, "Every damn day of the week!" "Then you should attend the same number of A.A. meetings that you planned to drink!"

James' plan to drink everyday is a perfect example of planned failure. When James invested the same amount of planning, time, energy, and money into becoming sober, he was successful. James drank for 50 years, and he was now planning for 50 years of successful sobriety!

I have a friend who is a very good salesman. He was always putting time and energy into get rich quick schemes. He was spending more time working on other projects rather then his real sales job. He was not even covering his business expenses. Over lunch one day he was complaining about another failed Internet scam. I challenged him to put the same amount of energy, time, money, and effort into his real job for one month. He agreed to the challenge! The next month, much to his surprise, his boss' astonishment, and his family's shock, he made salesman of the month. Today he is the regional sales manager for the company, and he loves his job. Mark Twain said, "Habit is habit and not to be thrown out of the window by any man, but coaxed downstairs a step at a time."

## Step # 2

You are already using the practice of The Rule of 52 naturally in many areas of your life; you just don't apply it in the right direction. Break life into manageable steps, and then take one step at a time. God's plan for each of us is to advance constantly, ever expanding, growing to become a success. God did not make His master design to fail; sin just wears us out!

Linking the idea of a **Sociogram** to the idea of a **Timeline** forms a **Sociogram-timeline,** or a sociological timeline of your life or a Time Machine. This time machine will track your big life events from birth to death.

Try to think of your own big life events, including: birth; learning to walk, talk, and play; early childhood; first day of school; first day of Junior high; first love/crush; first day of high school; first date/kiss; first car and learning to drive; first job; prom/graduation; first day of college; becoming a Christian; college graduation; real big boy job and/or military service; advanced degrees; getting married; more advanced degrees; first child; more children; death of parent; first grandchild; retirement; death of a spouse; old age issues; and death.

You may list as many big life-changing, earth-shaking events as you can think of to your list. When you list every big event that happens to you everyday, you will discover that you will still do more common and mundane life tasks than big events. You still go to the bathroom, talk, and eat more than all the big events in your life. Statistically speaking, life's big events add up to no more than 100 to 200, or less than .01% percent of your total life.

This means that the majority of your life is lived out in day to day tasks, not in big events. It stands to reason, therefore, that the majority of life's failures and successes are in the day to day details and decisions of life. Guess which ones you have to get right to be a success. The day to day choices is the glue that bind success to your life.

A high school student wanted to apply for a job, and I asked him an uncomplicated question. "What if the person interviewing you asked for your attendance record at school? Would you hire yourself based on your attendance record?" Day to day details make the big events successful.

## The Rule of 1 - Things You Do Once a Year

Things that you do only once per year can impact your life dramatically. Some examples are paying taxes, voting, reunions, annual check-ups, birthdays, anniversaries, Christmas and all other holidays, school starting and ending, and vacation. These events may start with conflict and end with problems.

These once-per-year events may all have personal and family conflicts, such as which relatives to spend Christmas with or completing your Income tax on time. All of the traditions that shape our culture and society create conflict in the family. Could you imagine Christmas without Santa or Valentine's Day without greeting cards and flowers? With each social tradition event comes success or failure. We unfairly judge others and ourselves by the amount of success or failure found in these once-a-year events.

As individual needs grow more abnormal, the abnormal wants become the larger list. Consider a Christmas wish list, an anniversary list, a birthday wish list; the drumbeat of the list goes on. The list never grows smaller or less complicated. Ask yourself if your life is less complicated today than when you were younger.

The world system sets up the western cultural Christmas season for family failure. This is how the system makes money off of misery once per year! First, think about how many parents are riddled with guilt and feel like failures because little Bobby did not get everything on his wish list. Secondly, think back to your Christmas as a child. How many gifts do you really remember? Can you make a list of the gifts you received? Think about this last Christmas season and make a list of the presents you received, or even the presents you gave. You may not remember the presents, but you will remember the arguments, conflict, guilt, and anxiety. Next, consider all the leftover lingering debt and residual family problems. The problems circle your family like a flock of buzzards.

The perversely abnormal world system manufactured all of these problems. God's gift to Christians is the celebration of the birth of His Son. The world system uses God's Son to market toys and tinsel. The manmade world system convinces society that our happiness revolves around once-a-year big events. The world system spends 52 weeks per year persuading you to spend money. Your debt is a measurement of the world's system success. Your ability to repay the debt is irrelevant to the world's system.

Don't get me wrong, I love Christmas; I just don't do the guilt and debt thing anymore. I spend my time investing in making my family happy. Happiness does not have to come out of my wallet. Making Christmas a Spiritual, Christ-centered reality is meaningful and a big part of Christmastime for my family. A benefit of being a Christian is Christmas has more meaning than money. If you are not a Christian then all you can offer your family is what is wrapped in a box and soon forgotten.

## The Rule of 12 - Things You Do Once a Month

For the most part, things you do once per month fall under tasks. Some of these things include monthly work reports, church meetings, paying bills, ordering monthly prescriptions, visiting relatives, service projects, washing the car, rotating the tires, and changing the oil. All of these are tasks and are necessary and routine. These tasks are the very things that make success. I change my AC filters once per month in the winter and twice per month in the summer because it saves me money and improves the quality of the air in our home. It also prolongs the life of the HVAC system. The same logic applies to changing the oil in a vehicle.

Once-per-month tasks are also a part of emotional success. I try to write letters to people I know and care about at least once per month. I do this just to let them know how much I love them and that I am praying for them. When was the last time you wrote a letter to someone you love? I know you just can't find the time. I am determined to not let people pass off this earth with out them knowing how much I love and pray for them.

Many of my friends have said the letter always comes at just the right time! I buy discount cards, print address labels, write an uplifting message, and, for the price of a stamp, I share my emotional love and strength with people who I care about. It takes very little time, but everyone likes getting mail other than bills. The light company is always faithful to write you. If you write to just one person once per week for 52 weeks, you will have written to all the important people in your life. **Remember that discipline is the refining fire by which talent becomes ability.** Charles Spurgeon writes, "I owe everything to God's furnace and hammer and His refining fire. With His mighty hand God shaped me into someone He could use."

# The Rule of 52 - Things You Do Once a Week

We will save this for the next chapter!

# The Rule of 104 - Things You Do On Weekends

Follow the money! This is how the cops catch white collar crooks. The paper trail does not lie. The same thing is true with the weekends. Track where you spend your time and money during the weekends. Weekends make up 3 ½ months of the total year. Most Americans spend their disposable cash in these two days of the week! According to national statistics, these two days account for almost all DUI's, alcohol related auto deaths, sports accidents, crimes, rapes, spousal abuse cases—the list goes on.

A recent study found that almost all suicides and drug related deaths occur on weekends. Another survey found that almost all final decisions for divorce are made over the weekend. The primary reason given was that this was when they had time to make the decision. The majority of all drug and alcohol relapses occur on weekends. Finally, almost 100% of all weight control diets that start during the week are broken on the weekends. On the other side of the scale, almost all weddings, baptisms, first communions, funerals, and salvations occur over a weekend. Most wedding proposals and planned child conceptions happen on weekends as well.

Our society has a light switch mentality. Compartmentalizing the work week from the weekend is not Spiritual. Compartmentalizing is the world's system of reducing the individual to a commercial product. Ask yourself why weekend papers are full of advertisements for the big sales. The world system discovered that if you pay people on Friday and give them Saturday off, they will spend all their money on stuff they do not need! God gave man a day off to rest, not to play golf or get caught up on paperwork. God also gave man this day to recharge his Spiritual batteries with a church family. The other part of the weekend is spent mowing grass, washing clothes, cleaning and cooking in order to get ready for the next week. Are weekend plans and tasks driving you or are you managing your tasks responsibly? **You could be in the task trap.** My definition of a trap is when you make a bad choice that produces the seed of consequence. Avoiding a *Task Trap* will produce desirable fruit and the seeds of excellence.

**Task Traps have a Merry-Go-Round effect.** When you get on the Merry-Go-Round you will not stop going in circles until you get off. All Merry-Go-Rounds are fun the first few times around then they get mind numbing. It is like starting a new job. The first few days are exciting; but after the weeks roll on, the job becomes just mind numbing work. What if you had to live your day to day life on a Merry-Go-Round? Your anger would build. The tune, "Pop Goes the Weasel" would drive you crazy and conflicts with others on the ride will ensue! **Trapped by Tasks** simply means that inanimate objects like laundry, paying bills, Sunday softball games and mowing the grass have now taken charge of your life. **The Task Trap** will always squeeze God out of your schedule. There is a reason people wait for hours to get on a rollercoaster ride. God's plan for success is like a rollercoaster. We have a starting point and end with lots of twists and turns along the way. The ride is fun and Christians always want to ride it again. If you are a Christian and your life's ride is not fun, then you might be in **The Task Trap.**

## The Rule of 261 – Things You Do 5 Days a Week

The 2 dominant features of our life are work and school! That's the plan! On the compressed timeline, we spend almost 9 months of our year working or at school, or both! Sin kicked us to the curb on that deal. Consider the time you actually spend really relaxing or on vacation. Many people brag about never taking a vacation, but in the same breath they say that if they had a million dollars they would travel. The reality is that God created man in a self-sustaining garden that was weed free, danger free, and no clothes necessary.

Upon man's exit from God's garden, the workday commenced. God is speaking to all of mankind in Genesis 3:17 - 19 when He says, *"The ground is cursed because of you. You will eat from it by means of painful labor all the days of your life. It will produce thorns and thistles for you and you will eat the plants of the field. You will eat bread by the sweat of your brow until you return to the ground, since you were taken from it. For you are dust, and you will return to dust."*

Talk about a hostile work environment.

## The Rule of 365 – Things You Do Once a Day

There are things we do everyday: eat, sleep, go to the bathroom, talk, learn, breathe, and the list goes on. There is one universal experience known by all mankind, in all generations. Most people rarely live a single day without this experience. Man's universal experience is pain, from our birth to our last breath on earth.

In Matthew 26:57, Jesus was betrayed by the religious people of his day. Jesus was also betrayed by his friend in Matthew 26:59 - 74. In these passages it is clear that anger and fear are part of the betrayal process. The primary reason that a person hides their shadows of life's pain is fear of judgment and of being shot while wounded. This is an abnormal reality, especially for Christians.

We all collect a little darkness each day. When our individual darkness is exposed to the light, others are repulsed by the darkness. Instead of embracing the opportunity to minister to those who have chosen to come to the light, the individual darkness is used to inflict greater pain. One of the reasons programs like AA work is because drunks are comfortable talking to other drunks. After all, that's who they spent time with at the bars. One of the main reasons for AA's success is it is a judgment free environment. Can you say the same thing about your church?

# Learned and Earned

We all avoid and resist pain. Count how many types of pain remedies you have in your medicine cabinet. Keeping people pain free is a multi-billion dollar business because pain is experienced universally by all men. Pain is man's greatest motivator, and it is also the greatest builder of individual emotional barriers and walls. Pain builds upon itself; it provides the bricks and mortar to build abnormal life walls. The mind-recoiling effect of pain constructs an individual wall or a prison around the mind, body, and Spirit. The wall is held together with emotional trauma that then forges fear, hate, hurt, and especially unforgiveness. The extremely heartbreaking thought is that the wall really does not keep the pain out. The wall only protects the individual from success and God-given normal reality.

The wall of pain is a closed system, like a rat cage. Pain, emotional waste, and inbred abnormal reality are kept inside the cage walls. The wall of pain is a retaining partition that allows the bitterness and anger to rot and fester until it is the composer of reality. Friends and family are let inside your walls of abnormality only when they submit to your life of abnormality. This is why the battered wife keeps living with the abusive husband, the boss keeps the drunk on the job, and the mother keeps letting her son hang out with the wrong people.

This is the merger of the drunk's individual brand of abnormality and the wife's normal reality and moral knowledge of right and wrong. The merger can only occur behind the walls of pain and in darkness.

This is an additional form of your Task Trap. Your construction project of pain teaches others how to build their own individual walls. Your children now learn to build their own walls of abnormality one abnormal brick at a time. The bricks do not go up all at once but 365 days per year.

## The Real Problem - Pain Is Involved in Healing

Pain is also involved in the healing process. We build the wall of defense against all pain, not just bad pain. Working out at a gym makes you sore, but it is a good sore. Even taking a band-aid off a scratch hurts. We resist pain even when we know it is good. This is why so many smokers know they need to quit smoking but don't; they are afraid they can't make it through life without the next smoke. A fact you need to accept is that there is pain involved in being successful.

When I was in college, I was a successful athlete. I also trained six hours per day, six days per week, and there was pain in the process. Today, thirty years later, I look like the Pillsbury Doughboy. I had to redefine my definition of athletic success. I go to the gym now for health and weight control. This is my new definition of success.

A key concept is that you and you alone are in charge of defining your personal success. God is okay with your definition of success, as long as your success aligns with His will. Zig Ziglar writes, *"You were designed for success. You were endowed with the seeds of greatness; but would you know success if it tapped you on the shoulder and gave you its business card?"*

## Step #3 - Change Your Perception

People become quite extraordinary when they start thinking about what they will do instead of dwelling on what is preventing their progress. When they believe in themselves, they achieve success. It is not a secret. How you perceive a problem is more important than the problem itself. If you begin by changing your thought process, you can change the world.

In scholarly circles, primary articles are also called original articles because they are the original sources for information. For mankind, the original information source is found in the book of Genesis. The first five chapters of Genesis cover all of creation, as well as man's original conflicts. This includes the first days of creation, first stars, first man and woman, and the first marriage. The first calendar is found in Genesis 2:1 - 2,

*"And the heavens and the earth were finished, and all the host of them. And on the seventh day God finished his work which he had made; and he rested on the seventh day from all his work which he had made. And God blessed the seventh day, and hallowed it; because in it he rested from all his work which God had created and made."*

With the act of creation, God created time itself. God organized it into a system of 7 days a week and 52 weeks a year. God called this time system good. He has never altered the original plan. According to astrophysicists, all time is measurable back to the beginning of time. The good news is that time has not changed from the beginning of creation. Time is clearly understood as an original creation of God, and the intention is for man to operate in His will. God's time plan for man includes *The Rule of 52,* the 5 conflicts, the 5 needs, and the 5 rules of the harvest all at the same time, starting today!

## How to Use The Rule of 52 to Write a Book

When I hold workshops, people ask me many questions about how to write a book. I guess they look at me and figure if I can write one, anyone can. Some of the questions include: "I have an idea for a book, but how do I get started?" "I started writing a book but I just can't seem to finish? How do you get across that bridge?" "How do you find the time to write?"

**The need is writing. The conflict is getting started, finding time, and finishing the book.** The answer is The Rule of the Harvest; you reap what you sow.

When I was a child, I had a neighbor who was a dime store romance novel writer. She was divorced, raising two children, and she made her living as a writer. She would get up each morning, put the kids on the bus, and go to work in her home office. Then she would sit in front of her typewriter for the next eight hours working; only taking two fifteen minute breaks and one half-hour for lunch. This was her schedule Monday through Friday. She cleaned and shopped on Saturdays and went to church on Sundays. Following this routine, she was able to write six romance 'dime store novels' per year and make a good living.

*The key to her success* was that she made herself write a minimum of 5 pages per day. In 30 days she would write 150 pages. I write 10 pages per week, which adds up to 520 pages per year, and I budget time into my schedule to write. If you just wrote one page per day that would be 365 pages per year. You can write your first page today.

I am amazed at people who are willing to tear apart a room searching for the TV remote instead of walking to the TV to change the channel manually. If you had spent your time writing instead of watching TV, you could have produced a 365 page book each year of your adult life.

## How to Use The Rule of 52 to Help Your Children

Children spell love T-I-M-E. If you spend 15 special minutes with each child each and everyday, this is over and above the child maintenance minutes. If you do it right, your overall relationship with your child will improve.

Maintenance minutes are those spent driving to and from school or practice, correcting, teaching, reminding, and watching. Quality minutes are defined as one-on-one time that you spend simply listening, loving, and visiting. Quality time is not the opportunity for an extra lecture or arm chair advice time. It takes hard work to put into practice and make a commitment to listen and love.

If you spend 15 minutes with your child each and every day in 7 days you will spend 1 hour and 45 minutes of individual quality time at the end of 52 weeks you will spend approximately 4 days of quality time.

*A key to success to remember:* people are more important than things. If you consider your child the most important gift in your life, then the child is worth at least 15 minutes of your day. DO NOT confuse activities with individual attention time. That's like confusing knowledge with action. Authentic success as a parent starts with budgeting individual time in your daily schedule for each child. Kids love for you to watch them at their big game. What kids need the most is for you to know how their day went at school and at practice. They do not need for you to get protective and fix everything; they just need you to listen. When you listen and value what your kids are saying, they will quickly discover that what they have to say is valuable.

## How to Use the Rule of 52 to Clean

Statistics state that average American families are simply overwhelmed by daily tasks. A typical family of 2 parents and 3 children taking one bath per day generates 5 dirty bath towels; which means there are 35 dirty towels per week or 2 - 3 loads of laundry. I am reminded of Lamb Chop and Miss Shari's theme song, *"This is the song that never ends, and it goes on and on, my friends. Some people started singing it, not knowing what it was, Therefore they continue singing it forever just because,"* repeating into infinity.

Try breaking all that laundry time into seven days like this: the last person to leave in the morning puts one load of towels in the washer, and the first person home puts them in the dryer. Things like socks, towels, underwear, dishrags, and workout clothes do not have to be folded and can live in baskets, ready to be used. Save the folding and hanging clothes for the weekend.

Each person takes 20 minutes per day and picks up/cleans their personal living space. Work in teams and let each family member choose which tasks they would like to perform. I hate doing dishes with a passion, but I love to dust, mop, and vacuum. If you leave it all for the weekend, you will end up washing only what you need for the next week while the rest remains dirty. Meeting one need at a time, you will meet all the needs successfully. Five family members working 20 minutes a day for a week equals almost 12 hours of total cleaning time. Now you have more free time, and you have also met a basic survival need of each family member by providing a clean, safe place to live. Conflict resolution and conflict avoidance have occurred, and there is minimal effort needed to clean the rest of the home.

# Education

Many people are qualified for management positions, but they run into the wall of education. Corporations often have a hard and fast rule: no degree, no job! You were the best salesman in the company for the last twenty years, but you can't become the sales manager because you do not have a college degree. Adding insult to injury, your new boss is a 25 year old recent college graduate with no experience. You train him and do his job *on top of yours* just to make the sales quota. I cannot express how many times I have heard that story from capable men and women. They say, "I wish I had kept going to school. I wish I had used my time wisely in school, but it is too late now."

"Horse spit!" is my reply to those statements! In Proverbs 9:8 - 10, wise old Solomon said,

*"Do not rebuke a mocker or he will hate you; rebuke a wise man and he will love you. Instruct a wise man and he will be wiser still; teach a righteous man and he will add to his learning. The fear of the LORD is the beginning of wisdom, and knowledge of the Holy One is understanding."*

Learning is a Spiritual event that God created man to use and practice. It is God's will that you are trained and educated. Use any Bible word search program and look up words such as, teaching, learning, and training. It will astound you how much God has to say about education. It is logical to assume that a continuous lifetime education is God's will, and since He gave the need to learn, God will provide the recourse.

When our family travels, we always visit colleges along the way. Our children grew up not asking if they would go to college, but where they would go. In Proverbs 22:5, Solomon writes, *"Train a child in the way he should go, and when he is old he will not turn from it."*

Applying The Rule of 52 to the problem of finishing a college education is simplistic. Traditional colleges are divided into semesters: Fall and Spring semester with two sessions during breaks. Applying The Rule of 52 to completing college looks like this: a student who only takes 6 hours per semester for all 3 semesters will accumulate 18 college hours. In 4 years the student will have 72 college hours, which is more than enough for an Associate's Degree. I know you think that is too slow. The question is what if you had practiced this system for the last three years? How would it affect your life? Remember, it is not how you start the race but how you finish!

During my first semester in college, I had a roommate whose home was Kermit, Texas. He was studying to be in the ministry so I called him Brother Frog. I enrolled in the average typical freshman academic courses while he took 18 + hours of PE, which I thought was stupid at the time. Brother Frog's grade point average at the end of the first semester was a 4.0, and my GPA was purely embarrassing.

Brother Frog received a lot of scholarship money and was certified to be a referee. He became a school referee for the entire intramural sports program. He made $25 per game and he pocketed as much as $500 some weeks. I share this story with every young man who wants to go into ministry. I advise them to get a degree in accounting, business, teaching, or something in which they can make a living. By the time they get to seminary, most ministerial students are married and have a child on the way. Planning for success makes you usable to God.

The apostle Paul wrote 14 books of the New Testament, and yes, my list includes the letter to the Hebrews. In my opinion, Paul collaborated with Barnabas who was a Levite scholar, which would explain the differences in the letter of Hebrews. Peter, who was greatly used by God, was an uneducated fisherman who dictated 1st and 2nd Peter and dictated the Gospel of Mark. John Mark was educated, and after his failed missionary journey with Paul, he returned to write for Peter. The point is this: God will use you to your maximum potential. The more prepared you are to be used, the more you will be used. Your prayer should always be for God to make you usable.

Remember that the evil one does not care what you are a slave to as long as you are a slave. The devil is not prejudiced. He wants you to be a slave to sin, and it does not matter what sin! If he can keep you from doing God's will, the evil one has made you his tool and slave! What if God calls you to serve with a small, rural church that cannot afford to pay you fulltime and you are enslaved by personal debt? Proverbs 22:7 - 8 states, *"The rich rule over the poor, and the borrower is a slave to the lender. The one who sows injustice will reap disaster, and the rod of his fury will be destroyed."*

## Let's Make Money with The Rule of 52

Let's start with a question for pastors: what would happen if you visited and did outreach with one new family per week? Suppose each week, for 52 weeks, one new family joined the church. If each is a family of 4, that would be 208 new members in one year. What would that do to the size of your church? Economically, if each new family gave $25 per week, then the offering for each individual family for the year would be $1,300. If they gave $100 per week, the total would be $5,200. The solution to success is not the building, programs, or VBS, *it is families.* All the programs will happen because the members will need more programs. The needs will always drive invention and growth. The solution to church growth is to invest time visiting one new family per week for 52 weeks.

The same idea can be applied to insurance sales, real estate sales, construction sales—really any type of sales. If you add one new customer to your existing customer base each week, what impact would this have on your bottom line?

An elderly carpenter was ready to retire. He told his employer, a home builder, of his plans to leave the home building business to live a more leisurely life with his wife and extended family. He would miss the paycheck each week, but he wanted to retire. The home builder was sorry to see his good worker retire, and he pleaded with the carpenter to build just one more home. The carpenter unenthusiastically agreed. Over time it was evident that his heart was not in his work. The carpenter did not pay attention to details. He wasted time and materials. His workmanship was substandard, and he was over budget. It was a poor way to finish a distinguished career.

When the carpenter finished his work, the home builder came to inspect the house. Then the home builder handed the carpenter the keys and title to the new home and said, "This home is my gift to you and your family for all your years of service."

What a shame! If the carpenter had only known he was building his own house, he would have done it all so differently. It is true that you have many facets to your life, but you also have 24 hours per day to get it right.

I am sure that many of you are familiar with Solomon's beautiful poetic passages in Ecclesiastes 3:1 - 8 that begin, *"There is an occasion for everything, and a time for every activity under heaven."* **But the deeper well and meaning** is Solomon's commentary on how we use our time that is found in Ecclesiastes 3: 9 - 15.

*"What does the worker gain from his struggles? I have seen the task that God has given people to keep them occupied. He has made everything appropriate in its time. He has also put eternity in their hearts, but man cannot discover the work God has done from beginning to end. I know that there is nothing better for them than to rejoice and enjoy*

*the good life. It is also the gift of God whenever anyone eats, drinks, and enjoys all his efforts. I know that all God does will last forever; there is no adding to it or taking from it. God works so that people will be in awe of Him. Whatever is has already been, and whatever will be, already is. God repeats what has passed."*

One of my preferred philosophers is Winnie the Pooh and I quote, "It is more fun to talk with someone who doesn't use long, difficult words but rather short, easy words like, "'What about lunch?""

Paul writes, Ephesians 5:15 - 17, *"Pay careful attention, then, to how you walk—not as unwise people but as wise, making the most of the time, because the days are evil. So don't be foolish, but understand what the Lord's will is."*

# Chapter 15

## Making Lists and Keeping Lists

Whenever I speak to a group of students, I often have them participate in the following activity. I ask them to take out a piece of paper, make 2 columns, and list 10 things that they have succeeded at and 10 things they struggle with. The list must be composed of personal successes and personal problems. Next, I take a piece of paper and place it on the floor in front of me and ask them to engage their imaginations. I say something like, "Use your imagination to picture that your family, friends, and the people you love are on the other side of this piece of paper, and their lives are being threatened. A cowardly terrorist is going to kill them unless you go to the other side of the paper and save them!" I over-exaggerate, expressing to the students that the paper is the only thing standing between terrorist and them. The piece of paper is keeping them from saving their loved ones.

Then I ask the students, "What would you do to the piece of paper?" before going around the room and listening to the student's answers. Some of the common responses are, "I would step over the paper." "I would go around the paper." "I would just tear it up and throw it away." My reply to the students is, "You're all exactly right!"

Next, I take the piece of paper and hold it up for all to see as I tell them, "I would never allow a piece of paper to keep me from saving my family. In fact, I would never allow any inanimate object to keep me from success!" Still holding the paper up for all to see, I state, "I would never allow the lack of a high school diploma or college degree to keep me from my success."

Consider that a degree is nothing more than a piece of paper. Can you imagine a piece of paper keeping you from feeding your family, buying a car, or getting a job? A math test or English quiz is nothing more than a piece of paper with a grade. Yet everyday I hear people say things like, "I wish I had studied more," or "if I only had a degree, then I could get a better job."

Then, being as disrespectful to a piece of paper as one can be, I crumple it up and toss it across the room into the trashcan. I ask the students to look at their list and decide how many people, places, and things are stopping their personal success. For high school students, success stoppers are things like boyfriends, girlfriends, not studying, computer games, not going to church, partying, injuries, the list goes on. My final question for the students is always, "What can you do today to overcome the success stoppers in your life? What can you do today? Make a new list of success."

My son Jonathan and I were planning our respective days over breakfast one morning. We both scribbled our to-do list for the day on our writing tablets. Jonathan paused, looked up, and said, "Life is nothing but a list." What an intriguing idea to think that mankind has minimized their existence and perspective of success down to a to-do list. Talk about reaching a new low. You have left your self-worth hanging in the balance of a to-do list, thinking that success is achieved when the list is complete. What a fantasy! Deadlines and commitments never end. Calendar dates drive us, and the list is never complete because there is always one more thing. Even when we die, someone reads about the list of our life in our obituary.

Americans have a list for everything: diseases, what to eat, what not to eat, gifts, holidays, birthdays, anniversaries, wishes, groceries, sales, honey-do-lists, agendas for meetings, packing, guest lists, points to discuss during the conference call, and even the list of things to put on the list.

*We also have lists that we use to control and manipulate others. These lists are formed from the substance of family conflict and lead to constant decay.*

**Questions you need to ask:**
1. Do I control my list, or does my list control me?
2. Do I use lists to control others?
3. Do I use my lists to hurt others?

If you do not fully understand manipulation by list, then consider the following explanation. Have you ever been in an argument with your spouse over dirty dishes, unwashed clothes, or anything else that is common? The conflict seems to escalate into a full blown angry argument. Your wife points to your failure to finish school and how horribly your mother treated her at Christmas six months ago. The conflict that started over the dirty dishes has now become a personal attack. The list includes all your many failures and faults from the past. Then she adds some statement like, "You don't love me and never did!" Now you are consumed with guilt and reply with something like "Well, if that's how you really feel, then why don't you just divorce me?" Now you are really angry and on the defensive, and you return fire with your own list of her past failures and disappointments. When the conflict subsides, you make a mental note to self: "Self, never share any fault or mistake with her again. She will only throw them back in my face and use them to hurt me." This is the point where trust and communication break down. Finally, you add the current argument to your list of her faults and mistakes. Ultimately, the list of conflict and decay is so well rehearsed and worn out that the list becomes a list trap.

Divorce papers always give a list of reasons for failed marriages. The chief among these is the legal term "Irreconcilable Differences." This is a summary of the husband's and wife's lists of unresolved conflicts. The divorce decree also has a list of divided property, assets, child support, and visitation. Now the court's list has added to your do's and don'ts. And it all began with just a sink full of dirty dishes.

**The key question is,** "Do you use listing as a way to control others and hurt others?" If yes, then the list is your master! The Rule of 52's plan is for you to rewrite your list. Go in a new direction, making a list of relationship success each and everyday.

Paul writes in Ephesians 5:18-20, *"And don't get drunk with wine, which [leads to] reckless actions, but be filled with the Spirit: speaking to one another in psalms, hymns, and Spiritual songs, singing and making music to the Lord in your heart, giving thanks always for everything to God the Father in the name of our Lord Jesus Christ"*

As silly as these verses may sound, it is often true that you are the happiest when you have a song in your heart and a melody on your lips. When you argue or have a conflict, you do not feel like singing, and if you do sing, it is only to numb the pain. This is the very reason Christians love to sing in church. Worshiping God with singing and music makes Christians feel good. It is also why lovers play their special song at their wedding. Paul is writing about you rewriting your list. A simple challenge would be to make a list naming every wonderful thing about the person you are in conflict with. Start the list with your spouse because if you are married, you have conflicts. If you want to know anything bad about me, just ask my wife; she is the real expert. Next, make a list of the wonderful things about your children. Select a different item from the list each week for the next 52 weeks and sincerely share it with the person you love. The thing has to be personal and over and above, "Nice touchdown" or "Good work on your report card." Those things are very important, but this list is about who they are as a person and how much they mean to you.

In I Corinthians 13:11 - 13, Paul writes a great list to explain how Christians should practice love. *"When I was a child, I spoke like a child; I thought like a child, I reasoned like a child. When I became a man, I put aside childish things. For now we see indistinctly, as in a mirror, but then face to face. Now I know in part, but then I will* *know fully, as I am fully known. Now these three remain: faith, hope, and love. **But the greatest of these is love.***"

I do not feel that a person can be a legitimate Christian without the practice of love. The question is, "When was the last time you told a loved one how great they are and shared some of the reasons why you really love them?"

## The Power of the List

One Friday, a high school math teacher asked her students to list the names of the other students in the classroom on two sheets of paper, leaving a space between each name. She told them to think of the nicest thing they could say about each of their classmates and write it down. It took the remainder of the class period to finish their assignment, and as the students left the room, each one handed in their papers.

On Saturday, the teacher wrote down the name of each student on a separate sheet of paper and listed what everyone else had said about that individual. On Monday, she gave each student his or her list. Before long, the entire class was smiling. "Really?" she heard them whisper, "I never knew that I meant anything to anyone! And I didn't know others liked me so much." All of the students made surprisingly positive comments.

No one ever mentioned their list in class again. The teacher never knew if they discussed them after class or with their parents, but it didn't matter. The exercise had accomplished its purpose because the students were happy with themselves and one another. Their senior year came to a close and the students moved on with life. Several years later, one of the students was killed in Vietnam, and the math teacher attended his funeral. She had never seen a serviceman in a military coffin before; he looked so handsome and mature. The church was packed with his family and friends. One by one, those who loved him took a last walk by the coffin. The teacher was the last one to bless the coffin.

As she stood near the coffin, one of the soldiers who acted as pall-bearer came up to her. "Were you Mark's math teacher?" he asked. When she nodded, he continued, "Mark talked about you a lot."

After the funeral, most of Mark's former classmates went to a luncheon hosted by the church. Mark's mother and father attended, and they wanted to speak with his teacher. "We want to show you something," his father said. He pulled a wallet from his pocket and explained that it was found on Mark when he was killed. Opening the wallet, he carefully removed a worn piece of notebook paper that had obviously been taped, folded, and refolded many times. The father said, "We thought you might recognize this."

The teacher knew without looking that the paper was the one on which she had listed all the good things that each of Mark's classmates had said about him. "Thank you so much for doing that," Mark's mother said. "As you can see, Mark treasured it."

All of Mark's former classmates started to gather around. Charlie smiled rather sheepishly and said, "I still have my list. It's in the top drawer of my desk at home."

Chuck's wife said, "Chuck asked me to put his in our wedding album." "I have mine too," Marilyn said. "It's in my diary." Vicki joined in as she reached into her purse and took out her wallet to show her worn and frazzled list to the group. "I carry this with me at all times," she said. "I think we all saved our lists." That's when the teacher finally sat down and cried. She cried for Mark and for all his friends who would never see him again. *Unknown Author*

**The door swings both ways.**
You can use your list for good or you can use it for evil, but each day you have to choose how to use the list.

**Start a new list and make every other word love.**

**The Master Question is:**
**"What can you do today to change?"**

# Conclusion

*"When one door closes, another opens; but we often look so long and so regretfully upon the closed door that we do not see the one which has opened for us."*

-Alexander Graham Bell

In James 1:16 - 17, Pastor James writes about how we fool ourselves. "Do not be deceived, my beloved brethren. Every good gift and every perfect gift is from above, and comes down from the Father of Lights, with whom there is no variation or shadow of turning." James is saying that you should not talk yourself into believing that this world and sin will give you any good gift. He is saying that good only comes from God, and he eloquently expresses that God does not change.

In James 1:18, Pastor James continues by saying that man is the most important seed planted by the God of Creation. *"In the exercise of His will He brought us forth by the Word of Truth (Jesus), so that we would be a kind of first fruits among His creatures.*

In Luke 6:36 - 38, Dr. Luke records Jesus' words as Jesus attempts to teach His disciples how to personalize The Rule of 52 and integrate it into their lives. Jesus spent His entire ministry teaching His disciples how to be successful.

*"Be merciful, just as your Father is merciful. Do not judge and you will not be judged; and do not condemn, and you will not be condemned; pardon and you will be pardoned. Give and it will be given to you. They will pour into your lap a good measure--pressed*

*down, shaken together, and running over. For by your standard of measure it will be measured to you in return."*

Dr. Luke's three verses contain relevant cultural truth that was clearly understood by the men in Jesus' day. Jesus had the unique ability of compressing truth into a few words, and His clear, simplistic style is filled with unparalleled Spiritual wisdom which will never be surpassed. Jesus concludes in verse 38, *"Give and it will be given to you. They will pour into your lap a good measure--pressed down, shaken together and running over. For by your standard of measure it will be measured to you in return."*

At first glance, this verse seems like a philosophical metaphor, but Jesus was speaking to a society of people who were experts in desert travel and trade. The people of the Middle East then, like today, were dominated by their oceans of deserts. Throughout numerous centuries they had developed many traditions and customs pertaining to desert travel and trade. Desert travel was not for the average traveler or common tourist. Over thousands of years, the camel trains that followed the desert highways developed a subculture with many social traditions. One of these traditions is what Jesus was alluding to in verse 38.

When a camel train was a day's journey from its final destination and would encounter another outbound camel train leaving a city, both camel trains would stop and make camp. The two camel trains would camp for the night, share a meal, and exchange information. The gathering was far more than a social get-together; it was more like a news flash. The camel traders would share information such as which water hole was dry; who was selling over-priced camels in the city; and if war, plague, or desert bandits awaited them on their journey. The next morning the camel train entering the city would give whatever grain it had left over as an offering of blessing to the outbound camel train. The extra food was intended to bless the camel train as it traveled into the desert.

This grain offering tradition has been followed for over 3,500 years. The grain is very fine and must be pressed down tightly for the journey. The camel train entering the city would pour their extra grain into the sacks of the outbound camel train until the grain ran over the sides of the sacks. Then the men would shake the sacks and press down the grain before adding just a little more. The blessing and sharing of grain by camel traders continues to this day.

Give and it shall be given to you. God's blessings shall be pressed down on you and compacted tightly into you. Jesus was personalizing the process of the harvest for His men. You reap what you sow. You reap more than you sow. You reap exactly what you sow. You reap each and every time you sow. You reap later than you sow. These are the unbreakable rules of the harvest. Each and every aspect of life is a planting and sowing process.

## The Little Baseball Player

A pastor friend from college called me in the early 1990's to ask if I would counsel one of his church members. The pastor shared some information about the family with me, mostly the good stuff. The family loved the Lord and supported ministries with their home, work, and leadership. Basically, they were model church members. The pastor explained that the family really needed some professional counseling at this time, and I agreed to help. The mother called and made a counseling appointment with me that day. She drove an hour and a half to meet with me.

The mother was a slender lady wearing an expensive, well-worn sweat suit. She had the lines of pain and distress etched into her face. I introduced myself and she immediately started talking. She never stopped talking. She nervously paced the office floor and never sat down, explaining she had to make a very important decision that I would need to make for her! After that alarming statement, I tried convincing her that making decisions was absolutely not the role of a counselor. I never got to finish my counselor psychobabble disclaimer.

Instead, the mother slammed down a picture of a young boy on the desk. The young boy in the picture was dressed in a bright canary-yellow baseball uniform. He had big blue eyes and a tough guy smile; one of those smiles that happen because your mom is yelling at you to smile for the picture while the baseball coach is telling you to look tough for the camera. The mother demanded that I look at the picture of the boy, saying, and "Look at this picture. My beautiful son is dying and I don't know what to do!" I immediately thought about my pastor friend who had recommended my counseling services and how he had left out this piece of information.

She continued to speak breathlessly. "He has a grapefruit-sized tumor growing in his head, and I don't know what to do. My husband and I have exhausted everything on medical expenses, including our life savings and retirement. We are going to lose our home. I have all but alienated my other two children; both are in high school, and one is a senior!" She looked down at the floor and said through her tears, "My husband and I probably won't make it either." She stopped talking only long enough to draw a breath. At this point, I knew better than to interrupt. She was going to finish her story. Growing angry, she said, "My family has served God! We built a room above our garage just for traveling missionaries. We house all the summer youth interns. We have given our money to God over and above our means for years. I am so mad at God! My baby is dying and he hurts so badly!"

With her fists clenched she stated, "That damn tumor is eating him alive. I haven't heard him talk for months, and he can't walk. He can barely see, and he won't eat. He is wasting away." "Look," she said, "I am on a short fuse and they tell me his time is up. I have to make a decision, and you have to tell me what to do. Don't tell me to pray about it because I am done with praying! I am prayed out and Spiritually burned out, so you pray if you want to, but I want a decision."

There was a long pause, and I finally asked, "What decision?" I asked the question thinking I could have her make her own decision. I was hoping she would decide for herself the decision she had to make. That's the counselor training thing to do. But the woman would have nothing to do with my attempt at redirection. The mother said, "I have enough money left to buy groceries and pay some bills for the month. The doctors tell me my baby will be gone by the end of the month, but I have another option. I can travel to Mexico City where there is a group of doctors who say they can heal my son. I need to know what to do!" She focused on me for the first time and then said, "You have to help me."

"I can't make any decisions for you," I said. "You have to! My high school children won't talk to me, my husband thinks I am crazy, and my pastor's a coward!"

I took a deep breath, like a breath right before jumping off a diving board, and prayed silently. You could call my prayer the counselor's prayer of panic. Then I said, "You can always get more stuff, houses, cars, and money, but you only have one little baseball player. If you feel this is the absolute last chance to save your son's life, then you need to take the chance." Then, very softly and with my most compassionate voice, I shared with her, "If it were my son, I would go."

No, I am not stupid. I know very well that the advice I gave her goes against all reason. Unfortunately, I have known many people who were victimized by such frauds. Unlicensed doctors in Mexico prey upon the dying with false promises of a miracle cure. I was purely thinking about all the guilt that this mother would carry for the rest of her life if she did not try to save her son. We regret what we don't do more than we regret what we have done.

Seconds after I told her she should to go to Mexico she stood up, thanked me, picked up her picture, and walked out. There was no goodbye or exchange of pleasantries; she just left. Several weeks went by and no news. I tried to call my pastor friend who had referred the family, but there was no news. On a Saturday morning, I received a phone call. It was the mother of the little baseball player. I listened silently as she shared her experience with me. She had followed my advice and traveled to Mexico City with her son. A dry lump rose in my throat, and my mouth was like cotton. She took a flight from Houston to Mexico City, and she could only afford one airline ticket so she held her son for the duration of the flight.

The mother had to conserve money when in Mexico City, so they traveled using the bus system. The third class busses are overcrowded with passengers and generally have standing room only. Riding one is like traveling in a third world country where the passengers ride with their livestock and bundles.

She and her son stayed in a cheap, low rent motel as close to the doctor's office as possible. She chose the closest motel so that she would not have to go very far when she carried the boy to the doctor. She made it clear that she never slept the entire time. She explained the horrifying, violent street noise that went on all night outside their room. She was afraid of the giant rats that shared their room. Sarcastically she said, "The rats would not have been so bad if they had split the rent." What little food she ate made her sick, and her son's condition worsened daily. The little boy was completely blind and could only grunt. He refused all food and only drank sips of cola. The mother paused to regain her composure and said, "The doctors took all of my money. They poked and prodded my son." She started sobbing. "They hurt my baby. After a week of hell, the doctors told me to take my son and go home because it was hopeless! They took my money just to tell me that my son will die!"

The mother was finally defeated, demoralized, and physically exhausted. She and her son made their way to the airport and boarded the first return flight to Houston. A well-dressed man in a dark suit sat in the window seat next to her and her son. She was holding her 8-year-old son like a baby in her arms when the man leaned over and offered to hold the boy so that she could rest. She explained to the man that her son would not go to any strangers, but as the words came out of her mouth, the boy lunged from her arms and into the arms of the man. The mother was startled at her son's actions, but she was so mentally and physical exhausted that she accepted the generous offer from the stranger. She knew her son would be safe because she had the outside aisle seat, and the man could not get past without waking her. The next time the mother opened her eyes, the plane was touching down in Houston. The boy was still asleep, and she did not want to wake him, so the man carried the boy all the way through the airport and to her car. The nice man helped her secure the boy in his car seat, and she thanked him over and over again for his kindness. While she fumbled with her keys to open her trunk, the man disappeared without a trace.

She started the car and began the long drive back home. While the boy slept, the mother was alone with her thoughts. She worried about her family waiting at home. She was apprehensive about having to share the new bad news with her family. She thought, "How many times does a person need to hear that a child is going to die?" She would now have to break the heart-wrenching news to her family all over again. At that moment, the little boy began to stir from his sleep. He looked up at his mother and said, "I'm hungry momma! Can I have something to eat?"

She gasped at the sound of her son's voice and almost wrecked the car. She was gasping for air and couldn't talk, so she pulled over to the shoulder of the road to recover. In a panicked voice she said, "You talked!" For months she had not heard his voice, only his grunts and moans of pain. She caught her breath, whipped the car around, and drove straight to the boy's doctor.

The mother charged into the doctor's office, carrying the child in her arms, and demanded to see the doctor. In just a few moments, the doctor was in the room examining the boy. He ordered x-rays and continued to examine the boy while waiting for the x-rays to be developed. Then the little boy's doctor called in another doctor. The doctors left the examining room for a while before the boy's doctor returned to the room alone. The doctor slapped the x-rays up on the screen and announced to the mother, "It's gone." Almost out of breath, she asked, "What do you mean it's gone?" "The cancer, the tumor, it's not there in his brain," the doctor said. "I don't know where the hell it went, but it's not in your son. It's a miracle." The doctor's expression changed from astonishment to frustration, and he demanded to know what they did to the child in Mexico.

The mother was in shock and could not speak. She looked at the doctor and said, "They did absolutely nothing, absolutely nothing!" Then the once-paralyzed child began to move on the examination table, sitting up under his own power. It was evident that the grapefruit-sized tumor on the side of his head was no longer there. She put her hands on the boy's face and then ran her fingers across his bald head. It was then that she understood and believed. Her son, who was all but dead, was now going to live! He was blind, but now he could see!

Over the phone she told me that she fell on the floor in the doctor's office and began to worship God with overwhelming passion. She did not care who was watching her or if anyone questioned her sanity. She pleaded for God's mercy and forgiveness for her anger with Him as she experienced inconsolable grief and shame for abandoning God for hate's sake. Then the next great miracle happened. She suddenly felt her son's little arms around her as he said, "Momma, it's alright." And in that moment she felt as if Jesus Christ was holding her in His arms. She remembered the Word of the Lord, just like Jonah did in the belly of the whale. Hebrews 3:12 "Do not neglect to show hospitality to strangers, for by this some have entertained angels without knowing it."

Today the little baseball player is grown and has his own little baseball players.

**The End of Your Failure**
and
**The Beginning of Your Success**
is to
**Follow The Rule of 52**
**Thus, as you sow, so shall you reap.**
*Your Obedient Servant, in the name Christ Jesus,*
*my Lord and Savior,*
*Dr. Tom Barnette*

# Thank You

I wish to thank the following friends and family for their inspiration and support and being willing to read, edit, and pray for the book. With their generous support and encouragement the Rule of 52 book and the Family Life Success ministry is a reality. Thank You!

Belinda Barnette
Kati Lott
Travis Gasper
Steve and Valerie Williams
Brad Bevers
Casey Cease
Dianne Hodge

Thank you for all your dedication and hard work!

*Your servant Dr. Tom*

*The Rule of 52* will allow you to learn to sow seeds in your life, harvest what you have sown, whether it was yesterday, last week, last year or from your ancestors!

This book inspires you to differentiate between your wants and your needs. It will bring tears to your eyes and laughter to your heart. It is filled with Scripture and folklore of the past.

*The Rule of 52* was an absolute joy to read. Gripping reality, belly-rolling humor from a perspective seldom seen. If everyone reads this book and only applied a portion of it to their lives, the world would be profoundly different. Dr. Barnette has brought a simplistic approach and easy to understand handbook of solutions to everyday common circumstances, which most people have never stopped to think about, much less apply to ensure a successful life.

The author/counselor, Dr. Tom Barnette breaks down our out of control, stressed out, pitiful, pathetic and hopeless lives into 5 areas, and explains how easy it is to gain control and be successful. He achieves this through sharing true life events that will clench your heart. This is a must read to understand who we are, that we are loved and there is hope. He does this through laughter, love, Scripture and real life events. A Wonderful Read!

*Steve and Valerie Williams, Servants of the Lord*

# Works Cited

Alcoholics Anonymous 1976. Alcoholics Anonymous World Services Inc. New York New York.

Barnette, Tom A. 1995. Single Advance Workbook. Katy, Texas: Fishermen Press

---. 2003. Foster Children Training Manual Survival Skills Life Gate Social Service Ministries

Carroll, Lewis 1871. Through the Looking-Glass, and What Alice Found There. A Core Collection and Reference Guide New York: R.R. Bowker Co

Carter, Tom. (1988). Spurgeon At His Best Grand. Rapids, Michigan: Baker Book House Company.

Cory, Gerald 1994. Theory and Practice of Group Counseling, 4th Edition. Belmont: Book Cole Publishing Company.

---. 1996. Theory and Practice of Counseling and Psychotherapy. Pacific Grove, CA.: Book, Cole publishing company

Dante Alighieri, Dante 1306 Divine Comedy. English, H.F.Cary.

Douglas, 1962 Bible Dictionary. Nashville, Tenn. Broadman Press.

Eight Translation New Testament. 1974. Wheaton, Illinois: Tyndale House Publishers, Inc.

Enns, Paul. 1989. The Moody Handbook of Theology. Chicago, Illinois: Moody Pres.

Enoch, Mary Anne 2007. Alcoholism: Clinical & Experimental Research,

Frost, Robert. "Stopping By woods On a Snowy Evening" The Poetry of Robert Frost Chicago, United States: Holt, Rinehart and Winston, Inc., 1969.

---. The Poetry of Robert Frost .Chicago, United States: Holt, Rinehart And Winston, Inc., 1969.

Glasser, W 1961. Mental Health or Mental Illness. New York: Harper & Row.

---. 1965. <u>Reality Therapy: A New Approach to Psychiatry</u>. New York: Harper & Row.

---. 1969. <u>School Without Failure</u>. New York: Harper & Row.

---. 1972. <u>The Identity Society</u>. New York: Harper & Row.

---. 1976. <u>Positive Addiction</u>. New York: Harper & Row.

---. 1980. <u>Reality Therapy</u>. New York: Harper & Row.

---. 1981. <u>Stations of The Mind</u>. New York: Harper & Row.

---. 1984. <u>Take effective Control of Your Life.</u> New York: Harper & Row.

---. 1985. <u>Control Theory: A New Explanation of How We Control Our Lives</u>. New York: Harper & Row.

---. 1990. <u>The Quality School</u>. New York: Harper & Row.

---. 2008. <u>The William Glasser Institute</u>. W.Glasser.com, Chatsworth, CA

Gonzalez and Richards. 2004. <u>The Privileged Planet,</u> Regnery Publishing, Inc. Washington, DC.

<u>King James1611 Bible Version.</u> 1976 Open Bible Publisher, Thomas nelson Publishers New York.

Lombardi, Vince Jr. 2003. <u>What It Takes To Be Number #1</u> McGraw-Hill Professional Publishing 2 Penn Plaza New York, New York 10121

National Institute of Mental Health National Institutes of Health Feb 17, 2007 Science News, Vol. 171, No. 7, Feb. 17, 2007, p. 104. <u>New International Version.</u>

<u>New American Standard Bible</u>. 1996. Chattanooga, TN: AMG Publisher. 1984, New York, New York. International Bible Society

Robertson, Archibald. T. 1931. <u>Word Pictures in the New Testament</u>. Nashville, Tenn. Broadman Press.

Schwartz ,Delmore Calmly, 1937. <u>We Walk Through This April's Day</u> New York, New

Tozer, A.W. 1989. Faith Beyond Reason. Camp Hill, PA. Christian Publications

# Works Cited

Wubbolding, R.E. 1988. Using Reality Therapy. New York: Harper and Row.

---. 1991. Understanding Reality Therapy. New York: Harper & Row

Dr. Tom Barnette was licensed to the ministry in 1980 by Houston's First Baptist Church. He is an author, teacher and Professional Christian Counselor and the Senior Pastor of Believers Baptist Church in Pattison, Texas. Tom been a host of *Vital Issues In The Christian Home* for the 105.7 KHCB Radio network for fifteen years. Dr. Tom Barnette is also the founder of the Family Life Success Ministry Workshop and radio ministry.

Tom received his undergraduate degree in counseling from Southwestern Assemblies of God University in Waxahachie, Texas. He received a Masters Degree in Counseling from Houston Graduate School of Theology Houston, Texas, and his Doctorate of Biblical Studies from Masters International School of Divinity in Evansville, Indiana. Dr. Barnette has specialized in professional Christian counseling, pastoral care, and Christ Centered Reality Therapy for over twenty-four years of ministry.

Tom's extensive years of family and addiction counseling have proven invaluable by breaking down barriers between secular and biblical counseling. *The Rule of 52* is truly holistic, fully integrating Christ centered Biblical absolutes and Reality counseling.

The results of *The Rule of 52* are practical, relevant, and user friendly with counseling guidelines and intake processes that allow any counselor to treat the mind, body, and spirit of each individual and family. *The Rule of 52* is a practical guideline for real success in the Christian home.

Tom is the father of three children: Tommie Alice, Jonathan Clayton, and LeeAnn Marie. Tom and his wife, Belinda, have been married for twenty-six years. A Barnette family favorite verse is,
*"And the Holy Spirit helps us in our weakness. For example, we don't know what God wants us to pray for. But the Holy Spirit prays for us with groanings that cannot be expressed in words. And the Father who knows all hearts knows what the Spirit is saying, for the Spirit pleads for us believers in harmony with God's own will. And we know that God causes everything to work together for the good of those who love God and are called according to his purpose for them."*

**Romans 8:26-28**
*New Living Translation*

**Family Life Success Ministry**
**P.O. Box 5441**
**Katy, Texas 77491**
www.drtombarnette.com

**199**